CREATIVE ACTIVITIES

CREATIVE ACTIVITIES

REBECCA RICE

With Patterns and Illustrations by
VERNA GRISIER McCULLY

THE PILGRIM PRESS
BOSTON

PRINTED IN THE UNITED STATES OF AMERICA
AMERICAN BOOK—STRATFORD PRESS, INC., NEW YORK

Creation

THE LORD GOD dreamed a dream, and thought, and planned,
  And from this dreaming, thinking, planning,
He made a world, and clothed his world with beauty.
He thought of lofty mountains, line on line of blue
And misty purple against the sky.
He thought of trees, with branches reaching upward,
And then he thought of little flowers and fragrant herbs.
He filled his seas with fish, and caused great beasts
Of every kind to roam his forests and his meadows.
Sun, moon, and stars created he,
And set the universe in motion;
And then created man.
Then the Lord God looked about his world, and saw that it was good.

DOWN THROUGH THE AGES men have dreamed their dreams,
  And found their joy in myriad creative ways.
In early times, the cave men scratched
Their pictures on bare walls of caverns deep;
Crude and primitive, they looked like children's art.
Then men began to chisel images of stone,
And model little figures out of clay;
Unfinished they were too, the first strange efforts of a stirring sense,
And yet they showed an inner striving toward the beautiful in
    form and tone.
On through the centuries, and men still persevered,
And striving, learned new ways of adding to the beauty,
Grace and comfort of their lives.
Now many years, men of skill have painted pictures,
Carved statues, worked in gold and silver,
Have written poems and stories, capturing their dreams in words
    or music;
Great cathedrals rise, monuments of vision, striving, love,
Their windows glow like jewels, every hidden part
A work of careful craftsmanship.

I N EVERY ONE OF US there lies a great desire
     To bring our dreams to concrete form,
To see a vision, plan, and bring that vision into being.
It is for us to keep alive the art and learning
Of the race, and pass it on, a priceless heritage,
To those who follow in our steps.
It is our duty and our joy to lead our children on,
That they in turn may find the joy that comes
From bringing dreams and hopes to life.
Lord of us all, Lord of Creation, grant that we
May look upon our handiwork, and see that it is good.

Worcester,   R. R.
Massachusetts

IN THIS BOOK

☆

PART ONE

HANDWORK IN THE CURRICULUM

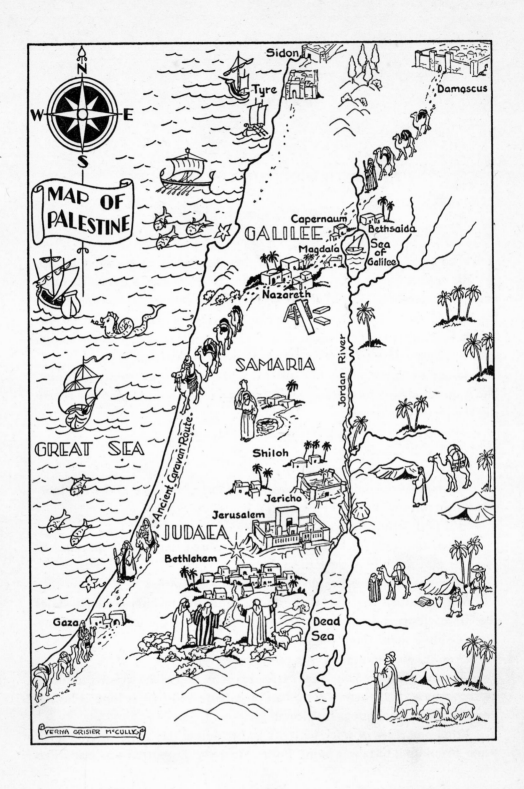

MAP OF PALESTINE

Sidon

Tyre

Damascus

GALILEE

Capernaum

Bethsaida

Magdala

Sea of Galilee

Nazareth

Jordan River

SAMARIA

GREAT SEA

Shiloh

Jericho

Ancient Caravan Route

Jerusalem

JUDAEA

Bethlehem

Dead Sea

Gaza

VERNA GRISIER McCULLY

PART ONE

HANDWORK IN THE CURRICULUM

THE STORY OF JAMES

JAMES WAS ONE of those children that we find in almost every group. His mother insisted that he come to church school each Sunday. He came only under pressure. Once there he determined to relieve the tedium of class for himself and for those about him by showing off. His teacher who was young and inexperienced was in despair. Finally she sent him to the leader, who was busy at her table preparing some work for later use.

James sat down beside her sullenly and she paid no attention to him. She went on sorting pictures. A few minutes later he was at her elbow watching the picture sorting.

"There's one you skipped," he said suddenly.

"So I did," she replied.

A minute later she was called away.

"Perhaps you would like to finish this job for me," she said. "I'm looking for pictures of Jesus when he was a boy."

"I'll find them," he said, and so he did.

When she came back the pictures she wanted were neatly arranged in one pile and the others were in their box.

"What are you going to do with them?" asked James.

She explained that the Come Early Club was making booklets about the life of Jesus and they were to use these pictures the following Sunday.

"Could I make one?" he wanted to know.

"Yes, if you come early," she promised.

The next Sunday James was there almost as soon as she was. He found to his amazement that there was no ban on talking and that as long as he was busy he could do about as he pleased.

From one piece of work he went on to another. He was a leading spirit when Friendly Town was being built. Then the suggestion was made that there should be a map of Friendly Town. The map was to be drawn in colored crayons on a large piece of cream-colored curtain cloth. James was eager to do it. After drawing a working plan on wrapping paper, listing the public buildings, placing them where he thought they should go, and discussing the whole matter with the leader he started in on the actual map.

Several of the boys and girls became interested; they were much impressed with his plan and wanted to help him, but he was in charge. He no longer needed to show off. He found he could be a leader doing worth-while things. He worked for weeks on the map, which became a symbol of a boy's change of attitude.

This led to other things. He became one of the leader's right-hand boys. Instead of disliking church school he came to love it, and through his interest in various activities he took his own place in the scheme of things. From a liability he became an asset.

Here was a bright boy who began by being bored. Given an interest, and something to do with his mind and hands, a chance to serve, he expanded. Under careless handling he might have developed a permanent aversion to church school and religion. Instead of helping his development, the school might have hindered it.

THE COME EARLY CLUB

ONE YEAR a group of children became so interested in their church-school work that more than half of them came very early. The group became known as the "Come Early Club." The children made two rules. The first was, "No fooling because it disturbs other people"; the second, "Find something to do."

One activity that the older members (third-grade pupils) were particularly interested in was the making of little individual prayer books. These were made of folds of wrapping paper and were about nine inches long and six inches wide. They were kept where the children could get them as soon as they entered the room. Also available was a large box of pictures clipped from Christmas cards, magazines, seed catalogues, mail-house catalogues.

As soon as a child entered he would get out his prayer book and write a prayer. Sometimes these would consist of only one or two sentences, and sometimes they would take up over a page. Some were lists of things the children wanted to thank God for, some were little stories telling God the things they felt he would be interested in. Some were prayer poems. Often the children would choose a picture from the box and write the prayer that it suggested to them. Others wrote the prayer first and then found a picture to match it. Several who liked to draw made their own illustrations. They took great pains to write well and to keep their books neat.

One morning six-year-old Marion came to the leader with a fold of paper and a picture.

"I want to make one, but I can't write," she said.

"Tell me what you want to say and I'll write it for you," said the leader.

Marion dictated a prayer and the leader printed it for her. Then she pasted her picture in and proudly took it to the drawer where the others were kept. After that she added a new prayer each Sunday, and other first-grade children followed her example.

One Sunday several children wanted to dictate prayers at the same time and there were not as many helpers as usual.

"I'll write my sister's for her," said one of the third-grade girls, and in a businesslike way marched her sister over to one of the little tables and wrote from her dictation, after which she wrote prayers for two other children. One little boy was not sure of what he wanted to say and the leader heard her making suggestions to him.

"I like to help them," she said, wriggling all over with satisfaction. "When I grow up I'm going to be a teacher."

It was a nice example of spontaneous co-operation between pupils and between pupil and leader, one of those experiences that make church-school teaching so infinitely worth while. One of the nicest things about the "Come Early Club" was the freedom of it. Children could talk freely to each other and to the leader. They could work together. Six or seven activities might be going on in the room at the same time, but there were never any disciplinary problems.

The children did not abuse their privileges. That extra half hour made it possible to carry out many activities for which there would not have been time otherwise. It totally eliminated the disorder that one finds so often before church school officially begins.

The prayer books were individual problems at first, but the interest of the children led to the writing of group and class prayers. The children also became interested in writing prayer poems.

"They sound just like real poems," said one child in delight.

"It's like making a puzzle," said another. "The ends have to match and they have to sound right."

Blessed with a pianist who was much more than mere pianist, one group of children who liked to sing made up the music for several of these prayer poems, and sang their songs to the department.

Another group was interested in dramatization. During the year they made up and acted several plays. They had one for Thanksgiving, two for Christmas, two World Friendship plays and a spring play.

A good teacher and leader will study the interests of their pupils, find out what they like to do and what they can do well and then give them encouragement and help in developing these fields of activity. One activity usually calls for skill in several lines of work.

ONE-HOUR PERIOD

IN SOME CHURCH schools the session continues only an hour. This is unfortunate, for there is so much to do and so little time in which to do it; but even in such cases the expressional activities should form an important part of the work. There are many worth-while activities which can be started at the church school and completed at home. Some leaders and teachers find time to meet their groups during the week after school. While a weekly meeting may not be possible to arrange, it might be possible to meet groups once a month, or at special times, such as before Thanksgiving, Christmas, and Easter. These midweek meetings work wonders in cementing group spirit and in making church-school work vital in the lives of the children.

There may be department and class activities. There may be activities by groups of two or three children, and individual plans. Leaders and teachers have no idea how many talents are latent in the groups they are teaching. We want to discover the abilities our children have and develop them, turning them into religious experience. A timetable that allows for interest groups is suggested below.

The first thirty-five minutes are devoted to a lesson and worship period by the leader of the department.

The last twenty-five minutes are devoted to different interest groups. One may be interested in music, another in dramatics, a third in the making of something connected with the lesson, and the fourth might want to practice memorization or creative writing.

The children may be divided into as many groups as there are teachers. Each teacher may work with the group for a month, at the end of which time there should be a Sunday devoted to demonstration. The dramatic group may dramatize the story they have been at work upon, the music group sing their songs, the creative writing group read their stories and poems; the object being, not to show off, but to share what they have done with others. The groups are then shifted to other teachers and new activities are taken up.

This arrangement is for the school where the leader is more experienced than his helpers in teaching the lesson, or where the helpers are specialists in various lines.

EXTENDED PERIOD

THIS PERIOD SHOULD be the most productive of all, for there is more time to accomplish the many things we have set out to do. First will come the leader's teaching period and the worship period. These may take half an hour or even longer.

Then comes the teaching of the lessons by the teachers. After the lessons the children form into interest groups with leaders who are experts in their own fields. The teachers of these interest groups should confer often with the superintendent and with the teachers of the classes in order to keep their work an outgrowth and enrichment of the regular class work.

To make this type of teaching successful it is very important that there be close co-operation between all the group leaders. Each leader should know the specific aims of the superintendent and should know the course of study in order that he may fit his own work into that plan.

THE CHILD'S RELIGIOUS EXPERIENCE

HANDWORK IS A DEFINITE and valuable part of the process of educating the child. This is one method of creative expression and deserves its rightful place in the curriculum. Handwork is no longer limited to drawing from a pattern and coloring, nor daubing color on a copy of some beautiful masterpiece. It is a program of enrichment, a supplement to the work that is being carried on in class. It is no longer handwork alone but creative activity unlimited in variety and scope. It is an outgrowth or an interpretation of the curriculum, and not something extraneous.

Very often the aim of a piece of handwork is to explain or make concrete some point of the lesson material that needs clarifying and to make it seem less strange and impossible. In telling or reading to children Bible stories and stories of life in other lands it is necessary to build up a knowledge of living conditions in those lands, so that customs which would otherwise seem strange to the children may be understandable.

It is said that there can be no impression without expression, and that in order to take something in, it is necessary to work it out. To learn to play the piano one must practice long hours. To learn how to do long division one must work out many examples. To learn how to be a Christian one must practice Christianity and follow the Golden Rule, establishing it as one of life's principles. One must learn by practicing thoughtfulness and generosity and love for others. Therefore we must give children opportunities to feel the satisfaction that comes from a program of worth-while activities.

Putting these principles into practice we make gifts both for those we love and for others who may not have as much as we have. We send home-made cards to those who are sick. We make up plays, songs and stories to share with our parents and with other departments, and all this comes under creative activity, or rather creative activity comes under all this as a means to an end and not an end in itself.

We do have to show children how to do things; but once shown how, they should be left to work out their own activities. Once they have mastered the idea and seen it in operation successfully they derive pleasure from it, and if a child enjoys doing something he is eager to continue doing it. If a child finds out it is pleasant to do things for other people he will want to continue planning gifts and services of friendliness. If he discovers that he can make objects with his hands, or draw well, or write acceptable stories, he will naturally enjoy doing these things.

A good teacher will have a goal in mind and she will have suggestions to offer, but the children should be encouraged to decide upon and carry out various activities. The teacher will prepare her work carefully, providing for emergencies, anticipating difficulties and being ready to avoid them. She will see to it that the right materials are at hand though the children may list these and help to provide them. If the teacher and group make their plans for several Sundays ahead this is possible.

The teacher will evaluate the plans made by the children and if they are trivial and not worth the time to be spent upon them, or if they are too difficult or in any way unsuitable she will have the final word as to whether they are to be carried on or discarded. Children and teacher will co-operate in carrying out the aims of the department as a whole and work in harmony with the superintendent.

Perhaps you cannot plan and practice and give a play. It might interfere with classes near you. There may not be sufficient room. However, there is no reason why your children should be completely cut off from all dramatic expression.

Many groups of children have made "movies," drawing each scene on a long strip of paper which is rolled and unrolled on short pieces of broomstick in a box. They may supply the dialogue as they operate the machine. (See page 97 for directions.) They may write the captions under the pictures. If they are too small to write easily—and the mechanics of writing frequently form a stumbling block to literary expression—the teacher may suggest that they tell her what to write under the pictures. The idea is the important thing.

Perhaps a group is at work making a Christmas crèche of plasticine. They come early to get under way, for in a school with an activity program time is all too short to accomplish the many things laid out to be done. They know where to get the material, for they put it away the preceding Sunday. Soon they are at work, chattering like magpies about their work, but in low voices, for they have learned by experience that others are at work and it is not pleasant to be interrupted.

In another part of the room another group is gathered about the piano with a leader, learning a new Christmas song to sing later at the service of worship. Other children who especially like to draw may be making a Christmas picture, a frieze or a poster. Some of the girls may be making paper dolls to send to the hospital or day nursery. The leader is there but in the background. She sees that everyone is doing something worth while, and is ready to help any group or child that needs her. The other teachers in the department are there to help children who are at work on some class project or wherever help is needed.

It is a busy, happy place because everyone has something to do that he or she is interested in. A person coming into the room will hear a hum of general activity, but it is not the sound of disorderliness one hears in a room where children are bored. The secret is to keep them busy doing things that are of value and of interest to them.

As the time draws near for group discussion the teacher may give a signal on the piano, or quietly pass the word from group to group that in a few minutes they will be called to the circle. This gives the children time to bring their work to a place where they can stop without disastrous results. They have time to adjust their minds to a change, and to pick up their materials and put them away. At the end of the stated time another signal is given and they take their places for discussion.

This is the time to evaluate the work which has been done, to show what different groups have been doing, to make reports, suggest improvements, and plan future activities. This does not take long. It is not difficult to pass naturally from this discussion to a prayer, for the children will be ready to thank God for the happy time they have had working together, for the chances they have had for making others happy, and to ask God's help in carrying out their plans. Thus the discussion period reaches its climax in worship. The children then go to their classes, coming together at the close of the session for song and benediction.

CORRELATION WITH LESSON UNITS

TO BE OF REAL value creative activities should correlate with the curriculum and supplement it, otherwise attention is divided and interest scattered. Much of the creative activity program is tied up with the seasonal plans; much should be planned about actual lessons. To help teachers in this correlation the following outline based on typical church-school units is offered. It is not comprehensive, but suggestive only. The units are those that occur in many courses of study.

Activities

A. *Activities Suggested for a Unit on the Life of Christ*

1. Christmas activities (see page 136)
2. Boyhood of Jesus
   a. Might-have-been stories
   b. Typical Palestinian home scene
   c. Stories for individual notebooks
   d. Illustrated map of the journey to the temple
3. Series of charts illustrating the following titles:

   a. Jesus Was Kind
   b. Jesus Worshiped God
   c. Jesus Helped Others
   d. Jesus Taught Others
   e. Jesus Was Brave
4. The frieze
   (Scenes from life of Jesus shown by famous paintings pasted on frieze with stories or explanations written by the children.)

5. Maps
   a. Christmas map
   b. Maps showing where important events in the life of Jesus took place
6. The Book About Jesus
   a. Stories written or dictated by children
   b. Group collection of poems, pictures, and stories

c. Original Christmas poems and stories
d. Christmas Book, a compilation of Christmas material from varied sources
7. Dramatizations
8. Miniature scene
   a. The Christmas crèche
   b. Home at Nazareth
   c. Easter scene

B. *Activities Suggested for a Unit on Our Church*

1. Miniature church or churches showing as close a replica of a children's church as possible, or several churches varying in size and architecture
2. Charts
   a. Chart showing the organization of the church, including trustees, deacons, minister, church school, choir, etc.
   b. Chart showing work carried out by church in other parts of the world
3. Model church service carried out by department after studying a church calendar

4. Pages from class book
   a. Picture of church and any of its activities either drawn by children or photographed
   b. Their own worship services for the period of time the unit is studied
   c. Accounts of service rendered by the department and any letters of recognition from Red Cross, Community Chest, etc.
   d. Drawings of worship centers, stained-glass windows, etc.
   e. Original poems, prayers, and songs for the unit
   f. Litanies
5. Illustrated booklet, "Our Church at Work"
6. Stained-glass window transparencies

C. *Unit on Joseph*

1. Posters
2. Frieze
3. Tent scene of Joseph's early home
4. Puppet (Joseph in his coat of many colors)

5. Clothespin dolls of characters in the story to be used for tabletop dramatization
6. Stories written by children
7. Map showing the course of Joseph's journey

D. *World Friendship Unit*

1. Paper dolls showing children of other lands
2. Illustration for books about children of other lands
3. Friendship litany
4. Friendship prayer for better understanding and respect
5. Poster
6. Frieze
7. Illustrated map

8. Exhibit of creative work of other nations
9. Gifts to be sent to European children for Christmas
10. Scrapbooks showing how much alike children are the world over
11. Scenes of other lands (diorama)
12. Letters to "Pen Pals" in other places
13. Gift boxes of church-school material, collected poems and pictures for southern schools that need them

CREATIVE WRITING. Many times needs arise for dialogue in a dramatization, prayers or litanies for worship services, written accounts of activities for the class book. Children may be encouraged to do this kind of creative writing. Very little children may dictate their prayers and stories to a leader. Older children will write them.

Using Bible verses for responses, the children may write litanies which are psalms of praise to be used by a verse-reading choir, or as parts of the worship service.

By letting the children contribute sentences such as, "For the beauty of red and golden maple trees on the hillside," and "For apples piled in glowing colors in the orchard," the leader will assemble enough material for a litany, in which the response may be, "We, thy people, thank Thee."

Children are quick to pick up the rhythm of the psalms, and like to put their own words into similar measured accents. Prayers, litanies, and free verse can be written by children with the help of a sympathetic leader. (See pages 14 and 128.)

PART TWO

THE SQUIRREL HABIT

A Litany of Thanksgiving

FOR the seed that the farmer plants in his garden,
For the rain that changes soil into plant food,
For the warm sun that ripens the corn and pumpkins,
Father in Heaven, we thank Thee.

FOR pumpkins ripe and yellow in the cornfield,
For rustling brown cornstalks,
For the long, warm days of summer,
And the crisp, cool ones of autumn,
Father in Heaven, we thank Thee.

FOR apple blossoms, pink and white in the springtime,
For apples piled in shining red heaps in the fall,
For apples stored away in barrels for winter's eating,
Father in Heaven, we thank Thee.

FOR purple asters smiling in the meadow,
For goldenrod making the wayside beautiful,
For the red, orange, and gold of autumn trees,
For the beauty round about that you have given us,
Father in Heaven, we thank Thee.

Choose as the refrain a simple verse from the Bible. Let the children mention various things for which they are grateful, and write the list on the blackboard. Then suggest that the class read the list again and add a few descriptive and color words. The next step is to rearrange the ideas, using the refrain at the end of each group. A class of girls and boys worked out the litany on this page.

PART TWO

THE SQUIRREL HABIT

T O CARRY on an activity program you will find a demand for many materials, but no department need lay in a supply of everything mentioned here. Except for basic needs, collect supplies as they are needed. It does pay however, whether you are teacher or superintendent, to acquire the squirrel habit, or the magpie habit, for a magpie collects whatever he sees.

If you are a superintendent it is your duty to be as useful and helpful to your teachers as possible. One way you can help is to establish a picture box. This should be separate from your picture file which contains mounted pictures you use in class and worship services. It should contain pictures cut from magazines and gathered from other sources which would be useful in making scrapbooks, illustrating Bible verses, and in making friezes. Old Christmas cards with pictures of the mother and child, churches and Wise Men are useful in notebook work and can be put into this box. Teachers and children should be encouraged to add to it, and all should feel free to take pictures they need when the need arises.

If you are a superintendent clip poems, stories, and articles from children's magazines and papers. Those you feel you can use paste into your poem collection or keep in your personal file. Others should be put into the common box for anyone to use in making notebooks and for scrapbooks for hospitals and schools.

MATERIALS AND EQUIPMENT

"A LITTLE BIT of ingenuity and almost any material will turn out a good pie," a woman of experience told the young bride. The possibilities of use for a great many different kinds of materials are almost limitless and often decidedly surprising.

"Anything from a clothespin to an old party dress is grist to my mill," one primary superintendent said.

Creative activity calls for varied supplies, and what those supplies are depends upon the nature of the project under consideration. It is surprising what materials can be salvaged from the home, and how many useful things will be donated if parents, friends, and relatives know what the need is.

There are certain supplies that every church-school department should have on hand if teachers use handwork to supplement their lesson material. Briefly listed these are:—

Paper
Pencils
Colored pencils
Colored crayons
Scissors
Rulers (¼ inch ruling for primary children and ⅛ inch ruling for juniors)
Erasers
Paste
Glue

Notebooks (optional)
A sturdy box, file, or drawer for each teacher
A large portfolio or envelope for each class
Paper clips
Gummed reinforcements
White and colored chalk
A file for pictures, poems, suggestions, etc.

If possible each child should have a pencil and a box of crayons. Valuable lessons in practical sharing and co-operation may be taught where there are not enough supplies to go around, but it does save time to have enough. If notebooks cannot be bought they can be made, using brown wrapping-paper, starch-paper or parchment for covers. New pages may be inserted as needed. It pays to reinforce the holes of notebook paper if loose leaves are used.

Each teacher should have his own box of supplies, and should notify the one responsible when more are needed; he should also have a portfolio, or file envelope, for pictures, verses, finished work and the like. The superintendent should have her own file of pictures and material. Each class should pick up its own materials and put them away.

Paper

1. Manila drawing paper. (One package, 9 x 12 inches will last a long time and is most useful. Order from a school supply house.)
2. Lined writing paper. (One package; ⅝th ruling for primary children, ⅜th ruling for juniors.)
3. One quire of heavy brown wrapping-paper. (Large sheets folded once, not rolled. This is most valuable for any number of uses.)

4. Box of white stationery. (Useful for writing letters to sick children, etc.)
5. Colored construction paper. (One package for each class. Useful in making greeting cards, etc.)
6. Tissue paper, white and colored. (Useful in making May baskets, flowers for miniature scenes, transparencies, etc.)
7. Black silhouette paper.
8. Blueprint paper. (Buy from store selling art supplies.)
9. Wallpaper. (Perhaps you can get a last year's sample book. Wallpaper is useful for making covers for booklets, backgrounds, design suggestions, greeting cards and the like. Left-over rolls are useful for making friezes. Use the backs.)
10. Curtain cloth. (Wonderful for friezes, maps, and permanent pictures. It erases without tearing or smudging, has a good texture for taking colored pencil and crayon, and does not crumple or tear. Get it through a mail-order catalogue if you cannot get it locally.)
11. Newspaper. (Torn into small pieces and soaked in warm water this makes a good material for puppet heads and relief maps; also for protection of tables and for quick aprons.)
12. Old magazines. (Often you will find usable pictures in them. Bright-colored advertisements can be cut in long triangles and rolled over a knitting needle to make beads for gifts.)
13. Crepe paper. (Costumes may be made of crepe paper. It is useful too in making miniature scenes.)
14. Paper boxes. (Houses, peep shows, movies, table scenes, decorated gift containers, castles, and doll houses may be made with a box as foundation.)
15. Paper towel. (For papier-mâché.)

Wooden Boxes

1. Cigar boxes for jigsaw work
2. Cheese boxes for window boxes, doll's furniture, etc.
3. Orange crates for chairs, bookcases, museum shelves, etc.
4. Doll houses

Old Clothes

1. Costumes for plays
2. Costumes for puppets
3. Furnishing doll houses

Unbleached Muslin

1. Maps
2. Runners for table
3. Crayon tapestries
4. Curtains for bookcase
5. Costumes

Clothespins

1. Clothespin dolls for sand table, miniature scene, and table dramatization
2. Four-poster doll's bed

Curtain Shade Cloth

1. Maps
2. Charts
3. Pictures
4. Time line
5. Movie scroll
6. Old Hebrew scroll
7. Covers for books and notebooks
8. Friezes
9. Scrapbooks

Colored Construction Paper

1. Greeting cards
    Thanksgiving
    Christmas
    Mother's Day
    Father's Day
    Convalescent

    For hospitals
    Appreciation cards
    Birthday
2. Cut-outs
3. Built-up objects
4. Boxes and favors

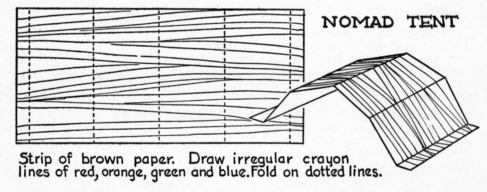

NOMAD TENT

Strip of brown paper. Draw irregular crayon lines of red, orange, green and blue. Fold on dotted lines.

Folded paper tents are used in a miniature scene of desert life

PART THREE

WHAT TO DO AND HOW TO DO IT

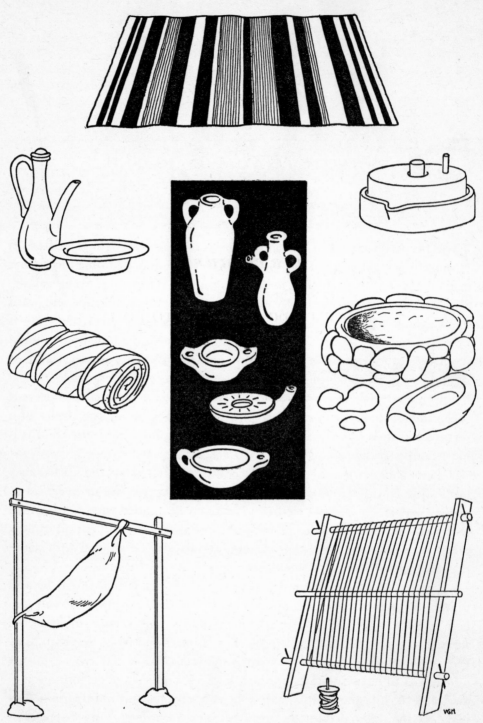

Objects for a miniature scene of life in Bible times: rug, ewer and basin, blanket roll, goatskin churn, water jars, dish, lamps, millstones, well and trough, loom

PART THREE

WHAT TO DO AND HOW TO DO IT

GENERAL SUGGESTIONS

PASTE AND GLUE. Glue should be used when strength is desired. It may be bought either in a tube or bottle. If it comes in a tube the teacher may provide a glass to stand it in when not in use. This will prevent leaking. She will show her group how easily glue comes out of the tube and warn them against squeezing it. She will also impress upon them that glue is powerful and a little goes a long way. If bottled glue is used the bottle should stand in a saucer and the glue applied with the end of a match. Children should be taught to lay the match down in the saucer and not leave it sticking up in the glue. This will prevent wasting the glue and will also prevent sticky fingers and messy work. By putting a little glue on one corner of a picture and then by bringing the corners together less glue is used and it is more evenly spread.

Paste is better for use by smaller children. Before class the teacher may put a little on individual papers. The children may pass in line to get these, or they may be handed out to them. Paste may be applied with match sticks. Rubbing the corner without paste on the one with paste will spread it more evenly and help to keep hands cleaner. Hands may be cleaned with damp paper towels at the end of the lesson.

In a department where much of this kind of work is done it may be well to have a number of oilcloth aprons as part of the equipment. It will also help to have either oilcloth covers for the tables or to keep a supply of old newspapers on hand for this purpose. The children should be taught to leave their tables clean and to put away their materials.

Plenty of elbowroom should be allowed for the sake of dispositions and discipline. While these hints may seem very obvious and unimportant they make all the difference in the world between an orderly, busy, happy class and pandemonium.

HOW TO MAKE APRONS. Creative activity, especially when it involves paint, ink, and other craft media, is bound to be messy work. Mothers send their children to church school in their "good clothes." It is only fair to the child and mother to protect those clothes from accidents. The best answer to that problem is an apron.

Aprons can be temporary affairs made of newspaper and pinned on or they can be made of unbleached muslin or oilcloth. The oilcloth ones are more expensive, but they will be more durable and in the end will pay for the initial cost. Two may be made from a yard and one third of oilcloth thirty-nine inches wide, as each apron can be cut from a piece eighteen inches by twenty-four inches. This does not include the straps. By getting different colored oilcloth, pieces left over from one apron may be used to decorate another.

If you stress the fact that these aprons are made on the lines of a carpenter's apron, you will avoid rebellion on the part of the boys, many of whom have the feeling that aprons are "sissy."

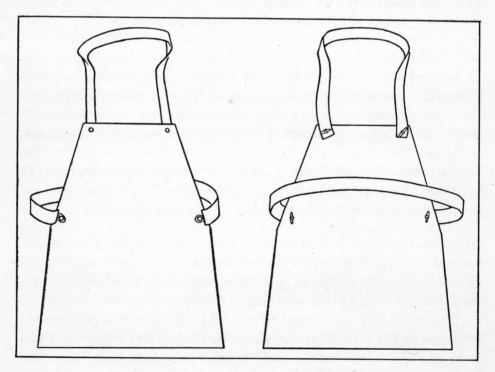

Aprons are made by both girls and boys

Materials

Pieces of oilcloth 24 x 18 inches, or newspaper, wrapping paper, or unbleached muslin.

Newspaper for patterns. (It may be well to cut patterns of various sizes.)
Buttons.
Loops of tape for lower buttons.
Needles and thread.

Procedure

Children pick out patterns according to size.

Pin pattern to the back of the material. (Children do this under guidance so material will not be wasted or defaced by too much pinning.)
Trace.
Cut out.
Measure and cut two-inch-wide straps. Length must be adjusted.
Sew straps to apron.
Adjust straps to fit the wearer.
Sew buttons to apron and sew loop buttonholes to straps.

Decoration

Applied decorations may be added. Cut patterns from left-over pieces of oilcloth, choosing colors that harmonize, and blanket stitch them in place. These may be put in a border along the bottom of the apron and along the bib, or one larger one may be applied to the bib. Decorated pockets may also be added.

This makes a good midweek activity or one for camps and club organizations such as Camp Fire Girls, Scouts and Four H. Third-year primary children can make simple aprons. Juniors can do more elaborate work.

THE HECTOGRAPH. A hectograph is a useful thing for a teacher or superintendent to have, especially in notebook work. Often a group of children make up a prayer or song which each child would like to take home. Sometimes they work out a play or arrange a psalm for choral reading. Frequently the teacher may wish to send notices, letters, or copies of work done by the children to their parents. Where there is not a mimeograph available, a hectograph is useful, and a great time saver. Of course hectographs may be bought, but homemade ones are very satisfactory.

Materials

A large, shallow, galvanized pan. This should be large enough to hold a legal-sized typewriter paper and should be about ¾ inch deep.

Three ounces of the best star glue. This comes dry and may be bought at the drugstore.

One pound of glycerine.

Seven drops of oil of cloves. This prevents the mixture from spoiling.

Directions

Break the glue into small pieces and place in an earthenware or enameled dish. Cover this with cold water and allow to stand overnight. In the morning place the glue in the top of a double boiler and heat until dissolved. Add hot glycerine slowly and boil for twenty minutes, then add oil of cloves. The mixture should then be poured slowly and carefully into the galvanized pan. Be careful not to leave any bubbles of air in it. These may be drawn carefully to the edge of the pan and broken. Be sure that the pan is resting in a level place so that there will be a uniform thickness of the gelatin pad. It will take at least twenty-four hours for this to harden enough to use. Keep in a cool place.

Usage

Use hectograph ink or a hectograph ribbon on your typewriter to make your first copy. Be careful not to make a mistake on the first copy, for hectograph ink does not blot and does not erase. Be careful not to get any of it on your hands or clothes, for it stains badly. Never let a young child use hectograph ink. If you want to reproduce a child's drawing, let him use pencil and then go over the drawing yourself with the ink. Mothers will not be happy if their children come home stained purple or green.

Write or draw the first copy on glazed paper. Use lined school paper or a good grade of typewriter paper. For copies use mimeograph paper.

1. Wash the surface of the hectograph with a piece of cloth dampened in cold water.

2. Lay a fold of newspaper over it to blot it dry. Soak up all drops of water.

3. Lay the original copy face down on the hectograph, taking care to place it right the first time, for you cannot put it down, then pick it up and

set it in another spot. Smooth it down, taking care that all parts of it come in contact with the gelatin pad. Leave it there for a minute or two and then, starting at one corner, carefully pull it off.

4. The impression is in reverse on the pad. To take off copies lay a piece of mimeograph paper on the impression, smooth it down carefully and then pull it off. Repeat this process until you have as many copies as you need. To keep the papers from curling lay them between the pages of a magazine or under several magazines.

5. As soon as the last paper is removed wash the surface of the hectograph with a cloth dipped in warm water. Do not use hot water, for this melts away too much of the surface. Be sure every bit of the impression is washed off, being careful to do nothing to scratch or mar the gelatin surface. Then blot the surface with newspaper and it is ready to use again.

USING COLOR. In arranging tableaux, making costumes for plays, and illustrating verses and stories children will be using color. Teach them that certain colors go more happily together than others, and that other combinations quarrel.

Let them discover this art principle by experimenting with colored papers. When giving appreciation lessons on pictures call to their attention that these harmonies are the result of consideration, not accidental. Appreciation of the beautiful enriches life, and enrichment of life is part of our religious program. Beauty is from God.

There are certain art principles which constitute valuable knowledge, and if practiced will result in more distinguished creative work which will be a joy both to its creator and to those who see it. Most children love color. We can help them to get even more pleasure from it by using it intelligently.

A color wheel and the formulas given below will provide a useful guide to the teacher. Only the most elementary facts are given. However, these pointers should be a help. (A color wheel may be obtained from an art supply store. Going clockwise, the colors are red, orange, yellow, green, blue, violet.)

Harmonies

The Monochromatic Harmony. Different values and intensities of the same color form a monochromatic harmony. This is apt to be monotonous unless strong contrasts are drawn, using black, white, or gray.

The Complementary Harmony. Colors opposite each other on the color chart are said to be complementary and using them together makes a complementary harmony. Two colors beside each other on the color wheel and their complements form a double complementary harmony. Yellow and purple form a complementary harmony, but yellow and yellow-green combined with purple and red-purple a double complementary harmony.

The Analogous Harmony. The best analogous harmonies are made by using one of the three primary colors—red, blue, or yellow—or one of the secondary colors—violet, orange, or green—with the color lying on either side of it. Suppose we start with yellow as the primary color, combining with it yellow-orange and yellow-green. The presence of yellow would hold them all together.

Neutral Colors

Black, gray, and white are neutral and can be used in any combination of colors for emphasis or to hold colors together. Outlining the details of a picture in black will work wonders in bringing each color out sharply.

Teaching Color

Much of this teaching is incidental. With little children one can list various pleasing color combinations on the board and simply tell them to choose the group they like best. Let them experiment on scrap paper, using different combinations.

Juniors are already experiencing the use of different color harmonies in public school and may have been introduced to the color wheel. If so they will be interested in using it to work out their creative projects, and will appreciate a color chart in the church school.

An appreciation of color in God's world may be worked into a project at any age level. Sunsets, autumn leaves, flowers, bird coloring assume new beauty and significance if looked at with a trained eye.

WORKING WITH PAPER

STARCH PAPER. Mottled paper suitable for notebook covers, and papers for booklets and for wrappings may be made, using wrapping paper and starch.

Materials

White wrapping paper.
One-fourth cup of starch.
1 quart of water.
Water-color paint.
Comb or cardboard designer.

Procedure

Mix starch with one cup of the water.

Boil the rest of the water.

Stir starch into boiling water, stirring constantly until the starch is clear and smooth.

Divide mixture and stir water-color paint into each part until you are satisfied with the colors.

Allow this to cool.

Wet wrapping paper on both sides and spread out flat on a table covered with oilcloth or newspaper. If there is a shiny side to the paper place this side up.

Place a tablespoonful of the starch on the paper and spread it evenly over the surface with your hand.

While this is still wet draw upon it, using fingertips for fine lines and fist or palm of the hand for broad sweeping lines. Scenes, flowers, undersea effects and an amazing variety of designs may be created by using various rhythmic motions of the hand.

Interesting designs may also be produced by using an ordinary comb or piece of notched cardboard for a designer.

Finished results may be stretched on newspaper to dry.

Tables should be protected by newspapers and children by aprons. Primary and junior children enjoy this activity very much.

FINGER PAINT. Much more satisfactory for the same purpose is the commercial finger paint.

This is more expensive, but it is more attractive as to color, texture, and result. It washes off easily.

When using finger paint give the children each a teaspoonful on a piece of wet paper at least eighteen inches by twelve inches.

Procedure for making parchment paper

Be sure they use fists and palms of hands for variety of line and stroke. Let them practice over and over again until they get something they really like.

Finger painting takes plenty of room so it is more practical for small groups under close supervision than for large groups. It is also better for a well-disciplined group that will follow instructions than for a less tractable group.

This is a good activity to try with music, for the music suggests rhythms that result in interesting pictures and abstract designs.

PARCHMENT PAPER. Parchment paper is especially good for making stained-glass windows. It may also be used in making valentines and cards for other holidays.

Materials

Tough typewriter paper or wrapping paper.
Water-color paints.
Crisco, Vaseline or paraffin.
A warm iron.

Procedure

Crumple the paper into a ball in your hand. Smooth it out. Paint over it with plain water, seeing that the whole surface is covered. While it is still wet drop onto it splashes of paint, letting two or three harmonious colors run together. Make sure that the paper is well covered with paint. Allow to dry. When the paper is dry, grease it and then iron out all the wrinkles. Protect both table and ironing board with several thicknesses of newspaper.

Color suggestions. Use colors which are side by side on the color wheel.

Leading for Stained-Glass Windows

Use black construction paper cut to the desired size. Warn the children to keep the border intact for the frame of the window. Encourage them to make simple designs as shown in the illustration.

There are three ways to cut the designs. They may be cut freehand after some newspaper practice. They may be drawn on one side of the folded paper, using white pencil or bearing down heavily with lead pencil, and then cut. The third way is to cut a design from newspaper, fasten it on the construction paper with paper clips and cut out the desired parts.

The parchment paper is fastened behind the leading and the whole hung in the window where the light may stream through. A window background for a worship center may be made for Easter or Christmas, putting an electric light behind the window.

SPATTER PRINTING. Wall hangings for the worship center and greeting cards may be made by the spatter-print method. This type of work is better suited to juniors than to primary children, for unless very carefully planned and carried out it is dirty work. The results are interesting and varied according to the selection and arrangement of subjects. As in any type of picture building certain principles of art in arrangement should be considered.

For Greeting Cards

Materials

Paper, either white or colored.
Colored inks, red, green, blue, brown, black, white liquid shoe dressing.
An old toothbrush.
Newspaper for protection.
A piece of window screen eight inches by six inches.

Procedure

Part of the picture will remain the color of the paper you use and part will be spattered, so you must warn your pupils of this and let them decide what their card is to look like when finished. Let them describe it to you. One might say, "I shall have a green tree on snowy background."

He would decide to use green paper and white shoe polish. The silhouette would be the tree and the background would be spattered. On the other hand he might cover the background and spatter a green tree on white paper. He must know what effect he wants and decide how to get it.

1. Cut the silhouette, taking into consideration relative sizes. (See page 103 for suggestions on cutting silhouettes.)

2. Spread newspapers under and around the work, and protect the children's clothes with aprons or newspaper.

3. Pin the silhouette to the paper which is cut to greeting-card size.

4. Pour about a tablespoonful of colored ink into a saucer.

5. Dip bristles of the brush into the ink and shake back into the dish any excess ink.

6. Hold the screen about six inches over the card and rub the brush across it. By moving the screen and keeping careful watch you will be able to spatter evenly.

7. Allow the card to dry thoroughly.

8. Remove silhouette.

9. Mount the card on a bright-colored mat for greater emphasis. This also gives a better finish.

You may want to use two colors. In this case you will be obliged to make two sets of silhouettes, each exposing to the spattering only that part you want single-colored. This should only be attempted after the simpler type of spatter printing has been mastered. Red and black spattered on white makes effective cards.

For Wall Hangings

Wall hangings make effective worship-center backgrounds, and if the designs have been worked out by the children as a result of experiences they have been having in class or in worship they are particularly valuable.

Materials

Cloth, unbleached muslin which has been dyed the desired color, or other firm cloth which does not have too glossy a finish.

If you are spattering on white choose a dark background color. If you are using dark ink spatter onto a light background. White on a dark background is more effective.

Colored ink or white shoe dressing, poster paint.

Newspapers for protection.

Aprons. (See page 22.)

Flit gun.

Beaverboard for backing to which the cloth and silhouettes may be fastened.

HE HATH MADE
EVERYTHING
BEAUTIFUL
IN ITS TIME

VERNA GRISIER McCULLY

Spatter print wall hanging and greeting card (center), and two silhouette slides

Procedure

For Nature Wall Hanging.

1. If a Bible verse or part of a verse is to be used cut the letters out of firm paper, having them at least half an inch thick. (See page 125 for alphabet.)

2. Pin letters to wall hanging, taking care to arrange them artistically and use enough pins to fasten them close to the cloth.

3. Arrange sprays of ferns, grasses, and finely cut leaves artistically on the cloth. Pin securely. Wherever possible pin edges close to cloth as this will give a more distinct outline.

4. Stand the Beaverboard erect against a well-protected wall or chair, for if it lies flat the paint drips and blots.

5. Fill the Flit gun with paint or ink, thinned to the proper consistency, and spray until all exposed areas of the cloth are covered evenly with little dots of paint. Each child should be given a chance to do some of the spraying.

Christmas scenes and illustrated Bible stories may be made in much the same way except that instead of nature sprays, paper silhouettes are cut by the children and pinned to the cloth, arranged to make an artistic picture.

MAKING BLUEPRINTS. Blueprinting delicate flowers and ferns helps us to capture their fleeting beauty. The print itself may recall in years to come a perfect summer day in the fields or woods, and so be a priceless memory of happiness. It may bring joy to someone else to whom it is given. It may awaken wonder in the heart of a child.

Perhaps the class is studying wonders in God's world, with special emphasis on light. Perhaps the children are discovering that what seemed an everyday common occurrence—the rising and setting of the sun—is really one of God's most precious gifts to man. Flowers, trees, animals, and people need the light of the sun in order to live. Perhaps experiments using light are being made by the class. The children discover what happens to a potato sprouting in a dark cellar, or compare the growth of plants in a sunny window with that of those shut away from the light.

Someone may have a new camera and the class has become interested in what happens when a picture is taken; they may make blueprints and see the effect of the sun upon sensitized paper. In working out such experiments we are encouraging wonder, and wonder leads, under skilful direction, to worship.

Some children have difficulty in making things with their hands. They never make anything that they can be proud to take home, and where there can be no satisfaction in a completed piece of work the child soon learns to dislike handwork. There are various reasons for this failure. Some children seem to have little artistic sense of balance, rhythm, form, and color. Some lack a co-ordination of muscles. Often the child who appears dull does much better handwork than the one who is brighter than the rest of the group. A nervous child has very little muscular control. Lack of success will soon discourage him, and dislike of the work follows discouragement.

Everyone can make blueprints if they follow the rules. The writer will never forget the expression on one child's face when she drew her paper out of the pan of water and looked at the Queen Anne's lace print she had just made. She had been doubtful about making a print, declaring over and over that she couldn't make a good one, but at last had been persuaded to try. Wonder, amazement, pleasure, and disbelief were all expressed as she looked up to the leader and said, "Did I make that? Is it mine?" It was the first time the joy had come to her of taking home something she could be happy over.

Uses for Blueprints

Blueprints make most attractive gifts. They can be mounted either in frames the children make themselves out of wallpaper or wood, or in frames from the dime store. They may be sent to the sick. The prints may be made into folders or calendars for Christmas. They may be presented to the minister and his wife, or the pianist or janitor in recognition of their services. They may be used in the class book, either to illustrate a page telling about the happy time the children had collecting materials and making them or for the cover decoration.

They may be used to illustrate Bible verses such as:—

1. The Lord hath done great things for us, whereof we are glad. Psalms 126:3

2. The earth is full of thy riches. Psalms 104:24

3. He hath made everything beautiful in its time. Eccl. 3:11a

Blueprints may be shared with children living in other lands or in different parts of this land. The emphasis will be placed on the idea of sharing some of the beauty we have with others. It may also be brought out that there are different kinds of beauty in all parts of the world.

FLOWER AND FERN BLUEPRINTS

Materials

Blueprint paper.

Sprays of flowers, ferns, etc.

A blueprint frame. A picture frame with glass and backer from the dime store, or even a plain piece of glass may be substituted for the frame. If you use the glass alone you will need a heavy cardboard or firm magazine for a backer.

A dishpan half full of water which must be changed frequently.

A pile of old newspapers or several old magazines.

Bright sunshine.

Clean absorbent cloth.

Buying Blueprint Paper

Blueprint paper is not expensive. It may be bought from concerns dealing in architectural or photographic supplies. It is more convenient if bought already cut, for cutting it is complicated work, but it is cheaper to buy a ten-foot roll and cut it according to the size desired. As it is extremely sensitive to light, this cutting should be done in as dimly lighted a room as possible and the paper should be kept face down.

As soon as pieces are cut off lay them between pages of a magazine. This keeps the light away and it also straightens them out. They can be stored until used, either in the magazine or in a large envelope between two pieces of cardboard. One roll should furnish enough for the use of two departments if they are not large ones.

Procedure

Gather all the materials you need. The day must be sunny and the more directly overhead the sun is, the better will be the results. Be sure that the pan of water is in the shade, however. You can work either out of doors or inside at a sunny window. Out of doors is more fun but it is convenient to have a worktable handy. Be sure the glass in your frame is clean. If you have previously pressed the specimens between the pages of a magazine they will lie flatter, but this is not absolutely necessary.

1. Arrange all materials where you can get at them easily. The leader should take charge of the blueprint paper and hand it out as needed.

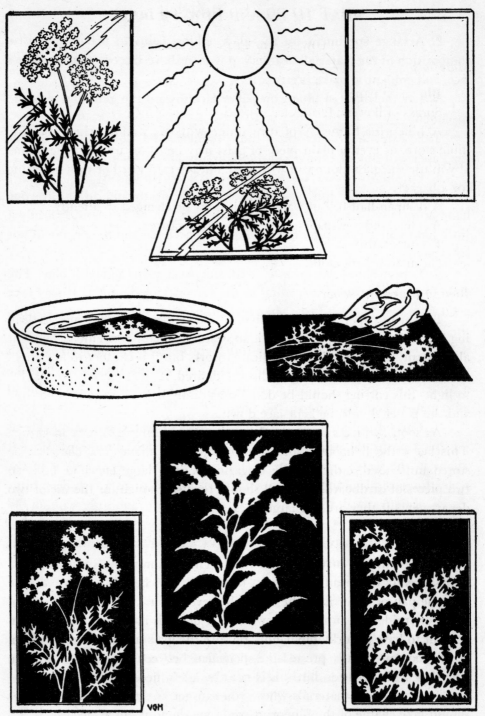

The day must be sunny when blueprints are made

2. Arrange specimens on the glass, taking pains to make an artistic composition of the material. Feathery grasses, milkweed seeds, Queen Anne's lace, and goldenrod make pretty prints.

3. Lay the piece of blueprint paper face toward the glass and over the specimen.

Take care not to disarrange the specimens, and work quickly so that the paper will not be exposed to the light any longer than is necessary.

4. Put on the backer, taking care not to let anything slip.

5. Expose to the full rays of the sun. Hold firmly and do not let your hand cover any part of the blueprint paper. If you do not hold it firmly a little light will get in under the edges of the specimen and the print will not be clear.

6. Expose about one minute or till the paper turns a grayish blue. The time of exposure varies according to the intensity of the light. It may take a bit of experimenting first. After several attempts one learns to recognize the light grayish color of the exposed paper when it is ready to be taken out. A delicate flower or one with very thin light petals does not need as much exposure as something more opaque. It is always wise for the teacher to make a print before showing the children how to do it. By so doing she is able to anticipate difficulties and to avoid them.

7. Carry the blueprint frame to the pan of water and as quickly as possible transfer the paper to the water, laying it in face downward. Move it about in the water to wash the chemical from the paper. Leave it in the water for several minutes, or until the background turns a rich deep blue.

8. Remove from the water and blot off excessive moisture with an old absorbent cloth.

9. Lay prints between pages of a newspaper or an old magazine. This prevents the prints from curling.

10. As soon as the print is dry trim it down to the best size and then it is ready to mount or frame.

PAPER CUPS AND BOXES FOR HOLIDAYS. There are many uses for paper cups and boxes. Hospitals and institutions use any number of them for tray favors for the holidays, and they are useful for church-school parties. May baskets can be sent to children belonging to the department, and to members of the congregation who cannot get out.

Paper Boxes

For little children the simplest type is the nine-square base. (See diagram on opposite page.) After this is folded, cut, and either pasted or punched for ribbon tying, heart ladies, flowers, baskets of fruit, Christmas trees, and other motifs according to purpose and season may be drawn freehand, or cut from colored construction paper and applied to the side or sides of the box.

Paper Cups

Muffin cups, such as one buys for baking, make satisfactory foundations for frilled, fringed, or rolled tissue-paper trimmings.

THE ROSE BASKET

Materials

Muffin cups.
Pink, red, or yellow and green tissue paper.
Paste.

Procedure

Cut strips of pink tissue paper.

Pull half of petal between thumb and table-knife blade to produce a rolled edge.

Do same on other side of petal.

After making several strips of petals wind them around the basket and paste into place, using enough to make a convincing rose.

Cut strip for leaves from green paper.

Push each leaf up the back of the knife blade to crinkle.

Paste row of leaves in place.

Braid strips of tissue paper to make handle and enough braid to paste around base of cup.

Chrysanthemums

Chrysanthemums may be made in much the same way, only instead of rolling the petals make them as the leaves are made, by pushing strips of paper between the fingers up the back of a knife blade.

"Heart Lady" and gay paper favors made with a nine-square box and muffin cups

Other Baskets

Other baskets may be made, using fringed or ruffled crepe paper. To ruffle crepe paper pull it gently through the fingers at the top edge, taking care not to tear it.

GREETING CARDS. There are many opportunities to make greeting cards in the church-school program. Bringing joy to others is one of our major objectives. Greeting cards may be sent to friends at Thanksgiving, Christmas, Easter, and Valentine's Day. They may be made for parents on Mother's Day and Father's Day. They may be sent to children in the hospital. In connection with Junior Red Cross work, children have made greeting cards to place on the trays of invalids in hospitals. This might also be done as a church-school project.

To get the most out of this type of work children should design the cards themselves, though sample cards and patterns may be shown to them as guides. The type of card undertaken depends upon the age and ability of the child. Very simple ones may be effective, while more elaborate ones may be made by those with more artistic ability. It is better to attempt cards simple enough to assure success.

TYPES OF CARDS

With Crayon and Pencil

Children draw Christmas symbols with colored crayons or colored pencils. Introduce them to the following principles of art:—

1. Spaces should be interestingly filled.
2. There should be some scheme of balance.
3. Rhythm is desirable.
4. Colors should harmonize. (Use neighboring colors on the wheel or colors which are opposite to each other.) Mounting these drawings on colored mats makes them more effective.

With Paper and Scissors

Simple and yet very effective cards may be made by cutting designs from colored paper and pasting them on a card. It is sometimes possible to find kits of gummed colored paper, thus eliminating paste. However, colored construction paper may be used. Children may either draw patterns

Greeting cards made with crayon and pencil

Designs may be cut from colored paper

Blueprints may be used with white ink lettering

and then trace around them on the colored paper or they may draw free-hand on the colored paper or cut out without a pattern. They should be encouraged to arrange their pieces in several ways before they paste, choosing the most pleasing design. Instructions in pasting are worth while before this lesson. See page 21 for suggestions.

With Blueprint Paper (See page 35)

Use silhouettes cut from heavy paper and proceed as described under directions for general blueprinting.

With Brush and Paint

Older children may make cards, using water color or tempera paint. If this is done each child should have plenty of elbowroom, a steady table, and some sort of protection for clothing. As this takes time it is an activity better suited for the mid-week session.

With Screen and Toothbrush

Spatter-print greeting cards are attractive and different, but they are messy to make. (See spatter-printing, page 30.)

With Linoleum and Knife

Juniors can make block-printed greeting cards and they enjoy doing it.

Materials and Procedure

1. Pieces of battleship linoleum cut to the size of a greeting card.
2. Tools for cutting. (A good set of tools containing a variety of cutters and two tools may be bought for a moderate price.)
3. Pattern. (Designed by the child on paper the size of the block print.)
4. Absorbent paper for prints.
5. A press or an old wringer.
(Prints also can be made by placing block and card on the floor and stepping on it. If the latter method is used protect the block by putting paper over and under it.)
6. A brayer. (This is a roll for spreading ink evenly.)
7. Block-printing ink. (The water-soluble kind is better for children to use.)
8. Glass. (A piece 12 x 9 inches is convenient.)

Draw pattern on paper which is cut to the size of the block. A border is useful in tying the design together. In making the pattern keep in mind that the parts printed are raised parts and the other parts will be cut away. By coloring the parts that will be raised, one can get an idea how the print will look.

Using carbon paper, transfer the pattern to the linoleum block.

Using the smallest cutter (number 1), outline all lines as deeply as possible, keeping a clear-cut edge on the raised parts. Go over once or twice, deepening and smoothing off edges.

Cut away the parts which are not to be raised, cutting in deeply enough so that none of the cut-away parts will show when inked.

Squeeze a little of the ink on the glass and run brayer over it until ink is smoothly spread on both brayer and glass.

Roll brayer over the block, taking care to get all the raised parts well inked. If any of the other parts show ink cut them away, taking care not to smudge ink on the raised parts.

If using press adjust strips of cardboard the size of the card and thumb-tack them in so that card and block will be in the right position. Lay absorbent paper between strips of cardboard and place the block face down upon it. Apply pressure. Be careful not to let the block slip or the print will be ruined. Re-ink each time a new print is made.

To use the wringer ink the block, lay the absorbent paper over it, smoothing it down with your fingers so that all parts of the paper touch the design. Put the block and paper between the folds of newspaper to protect the wringer and run through the wringer.

Prints may also be made by laying the paper on the inked block and placing it between folds of newspaper on the floor and stepping on it. Step with the ball of your foot on the middle of the block with as much downward pressure as possible.

BLUEPRINTING CHRISTMAS CARDS. Christmas cards may be blue-printed, and here again the making of these cards is fascinating enough for adults and simple enough for children. Christmas silhouettes may be complicated or simple according to one's ability and frequently the simplest ones are the most effective.

The leader should have several finished cards to show the children, for people work more intelligently if they can visualize a goal. These should be simple. Then, standing before the class and working slowly, the teacher may cut several silhouettes from manila drawing paper or wrapping paper. Much is learned through imitation.

Have a pile of old Christmas cards handy for reference, so that the children may help the teacher make a list of Christmas symbols suitable for use on cards. This list might be as follows:—

candles	Christmas tree
stockings	gingerbread men
fireplace	canes

Various children might be asked to draw pictures of some of these objects on the blackboard. Plenty of trial paper should be on hand, for the best results are obtained with practice. The teacher should direct the first cutting operation as follows:—

Fold your paper.

We are going to cut the flame of the candle first. What shape is a flame? (Let a child draw this.) If we draw a line from top to bottom dividing it in two, what will half a flame look like? Show me with your fingers how tall your flame will be. (The tendency is to cut it too small.) Watch how I cut mine.

Begin near the top of your paper at the fold. Cut down and out and around and back to the fold. Continue, keeping your directions as simple as possible. Show the children that they must not cut to the edge of the paper or their design will come apart.

Another paper is then given to each child and he is encouraged to make some other object. He is allowed to cut as many as he has time for. At the end of the period he spreads his designs out before him and chooses the one he likes best. His name is written on this and the best ones are collected and put away for blueprinting the following week. The children may be encouraged to make designs at home during the week and if they like something they have made at home better than their school work they may blueprint that also.

The following week if the weather is propitious the prints may be made at a sunny window. The pieces of blueprint paper should be cut the size of Christmas cards and the designs cut from paper the same size. Blueprints may be trimmed and pasted on gray or white card mounts, or can be used as they come from the frame.

For detailed directions for making blueprints see page 35. The only difference in making cards is that paper patterns are substituted for flowers and leaves.

The folding-cutting method is one of the easiest ways of making patterns, but silhouettes may be drawn freehand and then cut out, or there can be cutting without folding and drawing. One thing to remember and to impress upon the children is that only the outside shape shows in a silhouette. Features do not show, so profile is better when cutting out a human figure.

Thanksgiving, Mother's Day, Easter, and other holidays offer opportunities to make blueprint cards.

ILLUSTRATION BY DRAWING

TOO OFTEN DRAWING is considered just one type of busywork. There should be a definite use for every bit of drawing done in the church school and the children should recognize the purpose in what they do.

Drawing is an important medium of expression that children are using continually—in illustrating notebooks, in making friezes, posters, miniature scenes, and in many projects suggested by this book. Drawing helps a child to observe carefully. It brings to light distorted conceptions.

A child left to his own devices will frequently first draw a house, then a sun with a face in it, then a strip of blue sky at the top of the paper and another strip of earth at the bottom. This leaves a wide white area between. While teaching art is not one of our objectives in the church school, helping children to express themselves is something we are trying to do. A little guidance and help on the part of the teacher will be productive of more satisfactory results.

Each teacher and each superintendent should have a wealth of suggestive material. There should be helpful books in the library. There should be pictures in the picture file to be consulted, but not copied. There should be no tracing or drawing around patterns. The pictures should give the child a clear mental picture of what certain things look like. No one can draw a camel who has not seen a camel or a picture of one.

Old Christmas cards are valuable in suggesting ways of drawing horizon lines. Children should be shown how the sky seems to touch the earth.

It should be brought out that objects in the distance seem smaller than those near by. They should be taught to start with the most important thing in their picture and to place it a little off center. This center of interest should usually be the largest thing in the picture.

It is well for each department head or teacher to keep samples of the children's work from year to year, not to be copied but as a suggestion of other work and as a measuring rod to gauge the ability and progress of the present group. It will benefit the children also to see what other children have done. We are too apt to accept less from a child than he is capable of giving.

Small children should be given large paper for their drawings and arm motion rather than cramped finger work is to be encouraged. In both primary and junior departments the scenery for plays can be drawn boldly on large pieces of wrapping paper and later fastened to screens or thumbtacked up for background. Colored chalk makes a good medium for this type of drawing. The papers are laid on the floor or spread on large tables when being made. Colored crayons and poster paint also can be used. Here again the children should be taught how to handle their media and their clothes should be protected.

It is well to know several of the principles governing the composition of illustrations.

1. Margins should be wider at the bottom than at the top and side.

2. A center of interest is important and the eye should travel to that center of interest. It should be a little off center.

3. The horizon line should be either above or below the middle of the paper and never at the exact middle.

4. Keep the eye on the picture by having figures facing the center of the paper rather than away from it.

5. Keep the darker or more subdued colors for the frame. Use the bright colors to help spot the center of interest.

6. Encourage children to fill up their papers. Backgrounds are as important in design as figures.

These rules should be presented as they are needed.

"David and Jonathan are the most important people in our story," we may say. "Where will you put them?"

"Here is a big empty spot in your drawing. What can you draw there to help fill it out and make a more interesting drawing?"

Let the children suggest ways of improving and planning instead of telling them what to do.

Things to Draw

Illustrations of stories.

Greeting cards.

Paper dolls of other lands or of biblical characters.

Friezes.

Scenery for miniature theaters, moving-picture machines, plays, box scenes.

Illustrated maps.

Illustrated Bible verses.

Class book.

Reminders to take home.

Pictures illustrating any project that is being carried on.

Notebook work.

Gifts.

Charts.

Posters.

Pictures to decorate room.

THE FRIEZE. A frieze is a series of pictures drawn or pasted on a long strip of paper or curtain cloth that illustrate a story, a series of related Bible verses, or some unit of activity. The making of a frieze extends usually over several weeks. As children add to it their interest increases.

A successful frieze made by a third and fourth-grade group illustrated two of the *Bible Books For Girls and Boys.* The children chose pictures from the general picture box that illustrated the points brought out in the book. They pasted pictures on the frieze and wrote stories under them. This summarized the work done and was a constant reminder of the lessons learned. It gave the department something tangible to show when people asked what was being taught.

Wallpaper comes in a convenient form to use as a background. Wrapping paper makes a more durable frieze because it is tougher. Curtain cloth is very strong, and particularly good if the frieze is to receive a good deal of handling. Erasing does not harm it and colored pencils and crayons can be used on it without difficulty. A class that likes to draw may make their

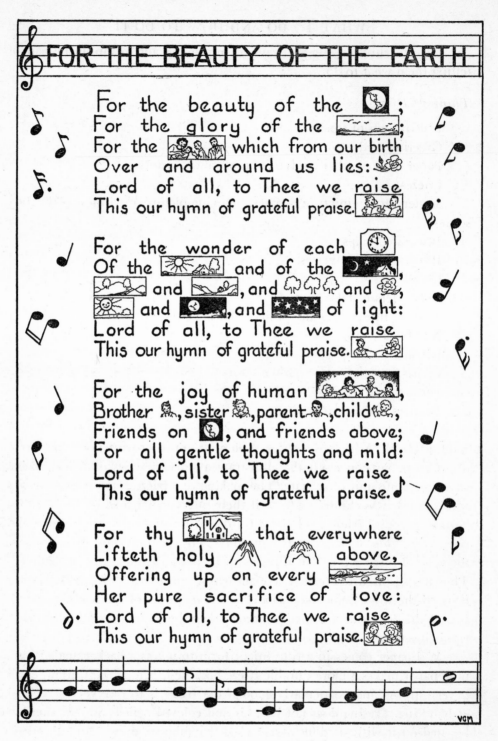

FOR THE BEAUTY OF THE EARTH

For the beauty of the 🌍;
For the glory of the ☁;
For the 👪 which from our birth
Over and around us lies: 🌸
Lord of all, to Thee we raise
This our hymn of grateful praise. 👫

For the wonder of each ⏰
Of the 🌅 and of the 🌙,
🏞 and 🌄, and 🌳🌳 and 🌸,
🌅 and 🌑, and ✨ of light:
Lord of all, to Thee we raise
This our hymn of grateful praise.

For the joy of human 👨‍👩‍👧‍👦,
Brother 👦, sister 👧, parent 👩, child 👶,
Friends on 🌍, and friends above;
For all gentle thoughts and mild:
Lord of all, to Thee we raise
This our hymn of grateful praise.

For thy 🏠 that everywhere
Lifteth holy 🙏 🙏 above,
Offering up on every 🏖
Her pure sacrifice of love:
Lord of all, to Thee we raise
This our hymn of grateful praise. 👫

Children enjoy finding pictures to be used in place of words

own pictures either directly on the frieze or on paper which is later pasted onto it. (See page 120.)

Suggestions

1. The Christmas Story
2. Thanksgiving
3. God's Autumn Plans
4. Boyhood of Jesus

5. The Story of Jesus as a Man
6. The Story of Joseph
7. The Spring Unit

RECORDS MADE INTERESTING

CHARTS. Charts express graphically many things. A good chart can be seen from the back of the room. It is bold in execution and brings out some special point. It may be the record of improvement or of work done by the department. It may tell a story or it may record attendance.

1. *Song charts*

Illustrated song charts are attractive and the illustrations help to clarify the meaning of words in a child's mind. The words of the song may be written or printed in large letters upon the chart with spaces left for pictures. Primary children especially will enjoy matching pictures to words. Having the words written where the children can see them will help to eliminate many of the mistakes made in singing the songs only by ear. The child who sees "goodness and mercy" written out will not interpret it as "good Mrs. Murphy," as one child did in learning the Lord's Prayer. Juniors enjoy illustrating hymns also and some take great pride in doing a beautiful piece of work.

2. *Class and Department Charts*

There are many activities being carried on during the church-school year both by departments and classes. Each department or each class may have its own record chart showing what it has accomplished, with a picture of the members of the class in the center. Arranged about this center of interest may be pictures and printed accounts of activities carried on by the group.

Children bring money to church school every Sunday as their offering or gift. The children should know where their money goes and they should be made to feel they are truly a part of the church and have a hand in carry-

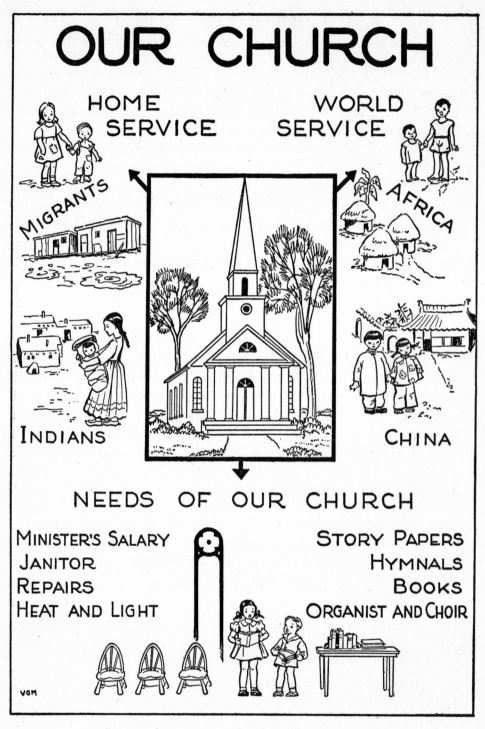

Interest deepens as work on the chart progresses

ing out its programs. To accomplish this graphically a picture of the church could be pasted in the center of the chart with lines going out from it. At the ends of these lines might be pictures and written statements explaining how the church or the church school uses the money that is brought in. One section might show the maintenance of the church and under it a list of things the church needs, such as minister's salary, upkeep of janitor, repairs, coal, heat, and light; another section, the work of the church in the foreign missionary field. The third group might show the home missionary field. In making such a chart the children would see the work of their church at home and abroad and themselves as a definite part of these activities.

Charts that record the doings of a class or of a department are growing things and interest in them deepens as they progress. Like the class book they remind children of happy events and accomplishments.

3. Birthday Charts

Get a calendar with the largest figures possible. Cut this up according to months and mount them in one large chart or frieze. As birthdays come along mark each with a gold star and the child's name. Another pleasant thing to do is to add a Bible verse for each child. To people who object to gold stars, may I say birthdays are red-letter days and these stars are not awarded as merits but are put on the chart to mark a shining day. This birthday chart is for beginners and primary children.

4. Rebus

The rebus is a chart which tells a story, using pictures in place of nouns. A rebus might be made showing what would happen if a strange child came to the class. First, on scrap paper, let the children write what they would do, or let them dictate to the teacher. Then write the story very plainly on the chart, using a picture in place of each noun.

5. Animal Chart (Primary or Junior Activity)

Materials

1. Large piece of heavy brown wrapping paper.
2. Pictures of familiar animals.
3. Drawing materials.
4. Pencils.
5. List of Bible verses suitable to the purpose.

HAPPY BIRTHDAY CHART

JANUARY

FEBRUARY

MARCH

APRIL

MAY

I was glad when they said unto me,
Let us go unto the house of the Lord.

JUNE

Give thanks
unto the
Lord.

Be ye kind
one to
another.

Let us love one another,
for love is of God.

Sing unto the Lord
a new song.

Oh, give thanks unto
the Lord, for he is good.

JULY

AUGUST

May you find joy in
bringing joy to others.

A happy smile, a cheery
word, and a courteous
tongue go with you.

May the new year be filled
with happiness and helpfulness.

The earth is full of the goodness of the Lord.

And Jesus increased in wisdom and stature, and in favor with God and man.

SEPTEMBER

OCTOBER

NOVEMBER

DECEMBER

Birthdays are gold star days

The children should suggest several titles and choose the one they like which should be printed at top of chart. If the group likes very much to draw animals, pictures may be drawn and colored; otherwise pictures may be pasted onto the chart. Under each picture a short story should be written explaining the provision which has been made for the winter for that particular animal.

Related Bible verses may be copied under the pictures.

6. *Other Charts*

Charts may be made showing life in other lands, among the migrants, on a southern plantation, or in a crowded city. The illustrations used may be either pictures from various sources or those drawn by the children.

For the department that likes to show visitors—parents, superintendent, or religious education committee—what work is being carried on such charts are extremely valuable. They speak louder than words and it is well to have a visible record of progress and activity.

CLASS BOOK. The class book is an illustrated diary recording the plans of the classes or of the department as a whole. For several reasons, it is one of the most valuable of all activities. It marks tangible evidence of progress, defines goals, and is also a reference book. The teaching process moves in cycles with much reviewing and recalling of past events. Children should share the feeling that both classes and department have a series of aims and plans and that they are all working towards a definite goal.

The first Sunday or two of the church-school year is devoted to getting acquainted and making plans. Children should be reminded of past work and asked what they would like to do in the future. These activities should be listed and later copied on one of the first pages of the class book. Such items as the following may be given:—

1. Have a play
2. Learn new songs
3. Vote money for the Golden Rule Fund
4. Keep a reading list
5. Make a poster
6. Make a model village
7. Make foreign dolls
8. Adopt a Chinese child
9. Make Christmas cards

When these plans are put into the class book space should be left so that others can be added. As each plan comes to successful completion it may be marked off with a check or a star. Pictures illustrating these plans

A class book inspires continuous interest

may be drawn by the children and taken home as reminders—pasted into individual notebooks or included in the department book.

As each activity is carried out an account of it should be added to the class book. Letters of acknowledgment for services rendered, gifts made, and letters received by the children should be pasted into the book. Copies of original songs and prayers with illustrations made by the children or cut from magazines may be included; also photographs of various activities, newspaper clippings, or any relative material. Sometimes an entire group of children will dictate an account to the leader and sometimes a scribe is chosen to write all the stories on scrap paper. After correction these are copied in the class book.

If it is part of our policy to bring out special abilities and encourage individual gifts, we should develop and use the aptitudes of our pupils. One child may enjoy creative expression and produce interesting and original stories and yet be an indifferent penman. Another may write beautifully but be painfully lacking in ideas. The good penman may copy the story of the other child into the book and both children should be given credit for the finished result. An artistic child may supply the illustrations. In this way three participate instead of one and each feels responsible for his part.

The class book lends itself to a great variety of expressional activity. There might be a copy of an original play, illustrated Bible verses, original illustrated stories. Group and individual prayers and original poems make the book richer and more interesting. Much of the mechanics of this work may be done by the teacher. Material may often be typed. This adds value in the eyes of children, saves space, and is often more legible than handwriting.

Samples of greeting cards, letters and the like may be included; also group photographs of the children at work make a pleasant addition to the class book.

One of the nicest things about the class book is the continued interest it inspires. "Do you remember this?" "Didn't we have fun at our World Friendship party?"

Class books may be made in a variety of ways but one requisite is that they be large, especially for the use of beginners and primary children. Heavy brown wrapping paper is a successful medium to use. One superintendent made books 18 x 14 inches, using folds of this wrapping paper.

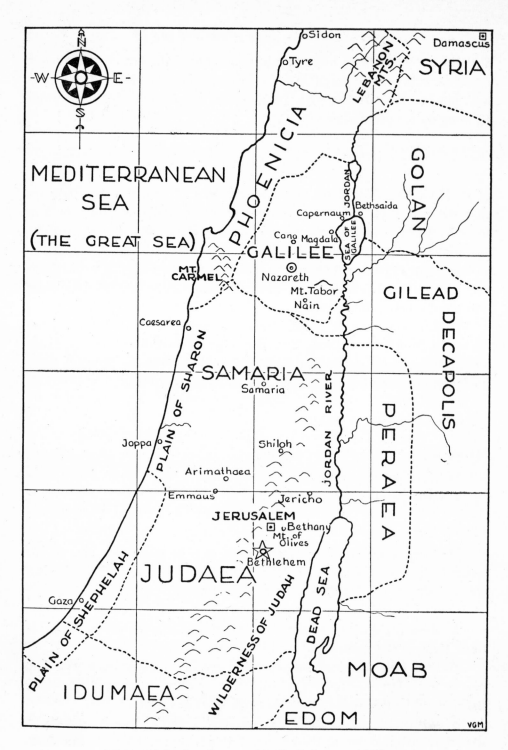

Map of Palestine drawn with the help of guide lines

She did not bind them together until the end of the year, so that pages could be added as required. Another way is to make them in the same way, but in loose-leaf form, the advantage of this being that the pages can be hung up for promotion day.

MAP MAKING

MAP MAKING USUALLY fascinates children. They enjoy making maps that are mere statements of geographic and historical facts, but they love to make the more imaginative decorative ones. Both kinds have their place. In public schools children usually start to make maps in the fourth grade, so the junior department seems the most logical place for this work. However, decorative maps such as the Christmas map can be simplified for older and more gifted primary children.

Outline maps can be bought from school-supply houses and maps can be traced from other sources. The map outline should be accurate. However, under careful supervision by the teacher and the use of guide lines, good maps of Palestine and other Bible lands may be drawn.

THE FOUNDATION MAP

Materials

Heavy paper or curtain cloth.
Colored pencils, lead pencils, ruler.

Procedure

Work slowly, developing this outline step by step. This part of the lesson is dictated, and directions should be followed exactly. The time for creative activity comes after the basic map is drawn.

1. Show the diagram to the children and explain the use of the guide lines. Explain the meaning of drawing to scale.

2. With ruler measure the paper and put in the guide lines. The map may be made larger or smaller at will, but keep the right proportion. Guide lines should be lightly drawn for they will be erased later.

3. With the children study the contours of land and water, and if possible develop a map on the blackboard. If this is not feasible make one show-

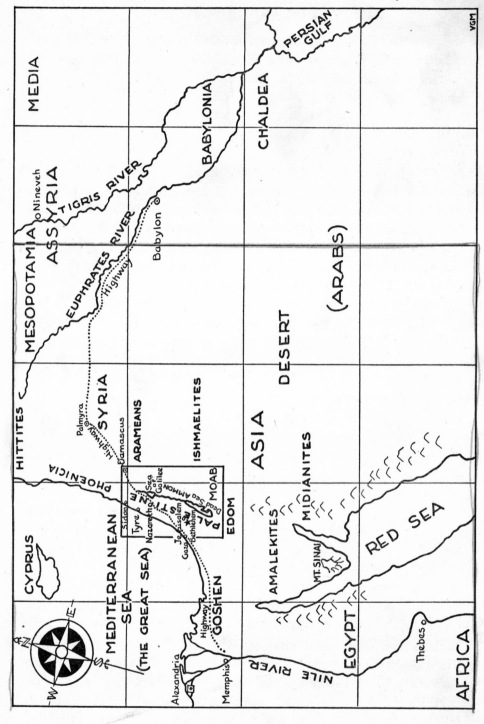

By estimating the relation of coastlines and rivers to the guide lines, map drawing becomes less difficult

ing the children where the lines should go, and have them sketch these in lightly. By estimating distance and studying the relation of rivers, coastline, and land masses in relationship to the guide lines, map drawing becomes much less difficult. Put in coastlines first, then rivers, seas, and lakes. If these basic outlines are accurate it is easy to add colorful details later.

THE PICTORIAL MAP. Using the foundation map as a basis various kinds of maps can be made. A favorite is the pictorial map. The Christmas map is a good example of this. The children locate Bethlehem, Jerusalem, and other places mentioned in connection with the Christmas story. They put a bright-colored borderline around their map, and mark in the places they have located. Bethlehem may be marked by a star. A small drawing of the Temple may be drawn for Jerusalem. The journey of Mary and Joseph to Bethlehem, the journey of the Wise Men, the journey of Joseph, Mary, and the child to Egypt, and later to Nazareth may be indicated by a dotted red line. The shepherds may be drawn watching over their sheep near Bethlehem, the Wise Men on their way to Jerusalem, and the stable at Bethlehem. Discuss the map with the children and let them make suggestions and carry out their own interpretations. This map may be made very attractive and decorative. (See page 2.)

Another way to make a pictorial map is by cutting pictures of shepherds, Wise Men, and the Family from Christmas cards and pasting them into place. This may be done by younger children or those for whom drawing is not easy.

Pictorial maps of the "Life and Work of Jesus," and Old Testament heroes may also be made. A world map or a map of the United States may be the basis of a pictorial map showing the work of the church in various fields. Here you would use an outline map and not try to draw one freehand with the guide lines.

THE BUILT-UP OR TABLE MAP. A foundation map is first made. This should be enlarged several times, and marked boldly with black crayon. Use a wrapping-paper background. While several children are working on this let others print small tags naming various cities. Others may be working on small pictures illustrating Bible stories. These should be done in bright color, cut out and mounted on heavy cardboard with backers so they will stand. Small pictures of palm trees, shepherds, sheep, oases, wells, the

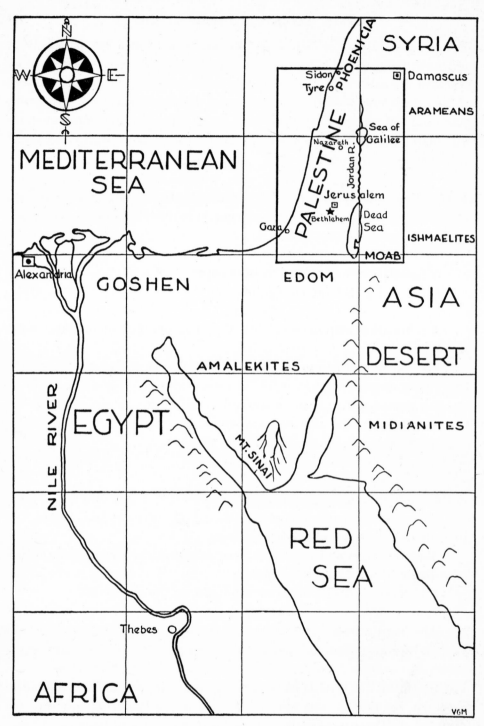

When basic outlines are accurate, details may be added

Temple, may also be added. These should be kept in a box or envelope, and form the basis of a game. Sides are chosen and a score is kept. The object of the game is to see which side is able to place the greater number of tags and pictures correctly on the map. Here is a map which is fun to make and fun to use later. A few minutes of play with this map frequently will help children to remember places and events more easily and agreeably than by drill alone.

THE RELIEF MAP. For older children who are learning how the surface of the land affects the lives of those living on it the relief map is interesting.

Materials

A foundation map drawn on blue paper.
A piece of glass large enough to cover it,

Or

A foundation map drawn on the top of an orange crate or other piece of wood.

Plasticine, or the modeling material mentioned on page 91 or the paper pulp mentioned on page 93.

Oil paint for the plasticine, or paint. crayons or water-color pencils for the modeling material and the paper pulp.

An orange stick, skewer, or lollipop stick.

Procedure

Place foundation map under the glass.

Spread modeling material evenly and thinly over the land masses, taking care to keep it out of seas and oceans.

Mark in rivers and lakes with your orange stick. Scratch down so the blue paper shows through the glass.

Add more modeling material and build up the mountains.

Paint valleys green, deserts yellow, and mountains brown.

This map is excellent for showing reasons for congested areas, and to explain caravan routes.

EMBROIDERED WALL MAP. Making the embroidered wall map is an excellent activity for the weekday session, for vacation schools, and for camp or club groups of girls. It makes a decorative wall hanging. An embroidered Christmas map would make a good background for the December worship center.

Materials

> Tan-colored sateen or unbleached cotton.
> Embroidery thread in various bright colors.
> Embroidery needles.
> Paper for patterns.

Procedure

Discuss the project with the girls and plan the map. What is it to be? How big shall we make it? What pictures should go on it?

Make a foundation map on paper, using guide lines. This avoids making lines which must be erased on the cloth. Transfer the map to the cloth. Mark in the location of places you want to mention.

Illustrate your map with pictures. Simplify into design symbols. Simplify these, and make them quite large and bold. The success of a wall hanging depends upon its striking quality.

Divide the work of embroidering the map between the girls. Use outline stitch. Embroider a black border. If desired there can be an inner border of bright red or orange, quarter of an inch from the other. Embroider rivers, coastlines, and seas bright blue. Then embroider the pictures and names of cities, using colors suggested by the pictures themselves.

Such maps can be made of Bible lands in connection with church-school work, or they can be made of the community or of camp. The more interesting the pictures, and the more brilliant the colors, the better the map as a wall hanging.

BIRD MAP (A Junior Activity)

Materials

1. A large outline map of North and South America.
2. Bird books for reference.
3. Pictures of familiar birds.
4. A box of colored stars.
5. Drawing material (optional).
6. Bible verses.

A prepared outline, such as may be obtained from various school-supply houses, will save time and will make a very nice-looking finished product. If it is impossible to get this, a map may be traced and transferred to brown wrapping paper.

Make a list of the birds familiar to the vicinity. Divide this among the children and ask them to look up the place where each bird spends the winter. These places should then be located on the map and marked with stars. Another star should mark the place of the church school. Dotted lines in different colors can mark the routes taken by the birds. Write the names of the birds on the different routes. Pictures of the birds may be drawn on the map around the border, or the pictures may be pasted on it. A brief account of what the map shows should be written and copied carefully in one corner. Bible verses can be added.

The more work that is done on the map the more meaningful it will be to the group. Be sure that the true purpose of making the map is not lost in the fun of doing it. Its purpose is to bring out the wonderful provision God has made for his birds. Some idea should be given of the long distances covered by such tiny creatures, and the wonderful sense of direction they possess.

MIGRANT MAP

Materials

1. A map of California or whatever section of the country is to be used.
2. Drawing material.
3. Reference material.

This activity should be used only if the children have become interested in the migrant problem, and are reading about it or doing something for a Community Center. It can be part of a larger project on learning more about migrant children and how we can help them.

Starting with an imaginary family the children trace their journey on the map from one crop to another, marking the journey with a dotted red line and illustrating various adventures on the way. Tiny thumbnail sketches and stick figures can be both amusing and instructive.

This map should carry a written explanation and it may also have a story written about the imaginary family. This should bring out the points emphasized in the lessons and discussion.

The neighborhood map is a happy reminder

of friends, good times, and trips of discovery

NEIGHBORHOOD MAP. In carrying out a nature project such as explor-
ing the wonders of God's out-of-doors, children like to make a map of the
neighborhood; putting into it where they live, the school, church, stores,
parks, and marking places where they have discovered evidences of God's
plan in creating a world of beauty. Much of the value in making this map
lies in matching these discoveries with appropriate Bible verses. This map
becomes a precious possession of the department.

Materials

1. Wrapping paper or curtain cloth 36 x 24 inches.
2. Colored pencils.
3. Bible verses pertaining to nature. Many of these may be found
elsewhere in this book. The Psalms are also a good source of this type of
verse.

Procedure

1. Discuss problems with the children, working out a list of neighboring places which should be included on the map.
2. Lightly sketch in main streets and important landmarks. These are
simply guide lines which will later be developed by the children.
3. Help each child to locate his home and let him draw it in its proper
place on the map.
4. Put in special features such as parks, lakes, gardens, and places
where the children have made discoveries.
5. Let them illustrate these discoveries with thumbnail drawings which
will be suggestive of their exploration.
6. Study a list of Bible verses with the children, allowing them to
choose appropriate ones to write or print on the map.
7. Color the drawings and outline them with black to make them
stand out more plainly.

Miniature Scene and Diorama

DIORAMAS ARE PICTURES in three dimensions, usually created in a
box or frame, and often having a curved background. They are becoming
increasingly popular in advertising and education. Dioramas are featured
in educational exhibits, and are often found in museum displays. The sand-

table work, used so much in the past, was based on the same educational principle. This has been largely superseded by the diorama and other varieties of the miniature scene which are cleaner to handle, take up less room, and are much more finished in appearance.

In building up three-dimension pictures we are carrying out a variety of activities. The background comes under pictorial expression and the planning and drawing of it should be the result of research and discrimination on the part of the children themselves. One gifted child, with one or two helpers, may do a large part of the background.

The making of figures, trees, houses, and other objects should be carried on by the group. Different objects may be chosen by the children or assigned to them. They should all be given opportunity to experiment with the final arrangement of the scene.

Materials for Diorama

A carton or large wooden box.
Shelf or wrapping paper for background.
Crayons.
Scissors.
Glue.

Procedure

Decide what scene you are going to make. Be sure that the aim of the group is worthy and that the activity ties up with class work.

Look up pictures for the group to study.

List objects which will be needed and look up how to make them in the section on objects for the miniature scene.

Have children make rough sketches of suitable backgrounds, and then let them choose one to develop. They may decide to use a combination of ideas. Cut the background paper to fit the space it is to fill.

Block in the picture lightly. Tell the children doing this to use a soft pencil and to make light lines which can be erased without leaving marks.

Color the background, letting the children use either colored crayons or poster paint. Outlining in a darker color brings a picture out and makes it more effective.

Glue into place. Cut a paper to fit the floor of the box and color it to fit the rest of the scene. Sand or earth may be used for outdoor scenes.

This makes the outer shell of the diorama ready. The objects and figures which you add depend upon the type of scene which is being made and the age and ability of the group. The scene may be lighted by a concealed flashlight or an electric light on an extension wire.

SHELF SCENE. Shelves, either in an unused bookcase or china closet, make ideal backgrounds for the built-up scene. Here the background is cut to fit the back and sides of the shelf and the figures are arranged before it.

The Three-part Cardboard Backer

Cut three pieces of very heavy cardboard, corrugated paper or plywood. The middle piece may be two feet long and a foot high, the side pieces one foot square. Hinge these together, using Scotch tape or string laced through holes along the sides. Use small hinges for wooden backers.

Make slip covers of shelf paper or wrapping paper to cover these. The background scenery is drawn on the slip cover. These backers may be used over and over again by making new slip covers for each scene.

SHADOW PICTURES. Beautiful effects may be produced by hanging several layers of colored gauze in front of the diorama and throwing light upon the figures from the side or rear. Mosquito netting can be tinted with various colored soap dyes. Choose colors that fit the scene. Rose, blue, and violet give a mystic effect to a Christmas crèche. Blue and violet might be used for a night scene. Orange and yellow would add to an autumn scene, or to a desert scene. Sheets of colored cellophane may be fastened over the front of a diorama also to give a bit of illusion.

The real effectiveness of all this depends largely on the colors used in making the figures. If gauze or cellophane is used the colors inside should be more vivid and more clearly outlined with black than if the gauze is not used. It is also more important that some type of lighting be used.

USE OF THE MINIATURE SCENE

1. Illustrating Bible Stories

The Christmas crèche.
Scenes from the life of Jesus.
(A picture of Jesus may be substituted for a child-made figure.)
Scenes from the life of Joseph or whichever hero is being studied.

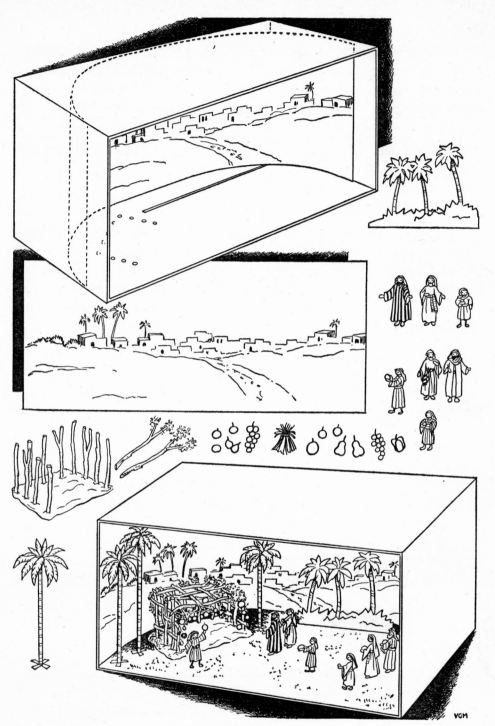

Diorama of the Feast of Booths

2. *Life in Bible Times*

Tent life.
Village life.

3. *World Friendship Scenes*

Illustrations from various books on world friendship the children are reading.
Life in other lands.
Migrant life.

4. *Seasonal scenes illustrating the Bible verse, "He hath made everything beautiful in its time."*

People for the Miniature Scene

PAPER FIGURES

Materials

Paper.
Colored pencils.
Paste.
Cardboard.

Procedure

Draw or trace figures of people onto white drawing paper.
Color.
Mount on cardboard and place under weights until they are dry.
Cut out figures.
Make backers of cardboard, spools, or wooden blocks and fasten figures to backers.

PLYWOOD FIGURES

Materials

Pattern. (Drawn freehand or traced.)
Thin plywood.
Poster paint.

Miniature scene of an African village

Shellac.

Jig saw.

Backers.

Sandpaper.

Procedure

Make pattern.

Trace figure onto the plywood.

Cut out figure with jig saw.

Sandpaper rough edges until smooth.

Paint figures with poster paint.

Shellac. (Try out shellac on poster paint before shellacking figures because some colors run. If the colors run omit shellacking.)

Fasten figures to backers.

PAPIER-MÂCHÉ FIGURES. (See page 93.)

PAPER DOLLS. (See page 89.)

CLOTHESPIN FIGURES

Materials

Clothespins.

Cornstarch modeling material for head (see page 91) or papier-mâché head. Bits of suitable colored cloth or crepe paper for clothing.

Pipe cleaners for arms.

Procedure

Model head of either the modeling material or papier-mâché, fitting it over the top of the clothespin.

Tie pipe cleaner to neck and bend into the proper shape for shoulders and arms. Allow head to dry. This will take several days.

Start work on costume. This depends upon the type of doll you are making. A simple kimono pattern for the woman's dress makes a good foundation, to which you can add gay skirts and aprons for the peasant doll, white apron and kerchief for Pilgrim, etc.

Men's clothes are more difficult. The best way to make these is to build them onto the clothespin, using the papier-mâché method, and when dry, to paint them with poster paint and shellac.

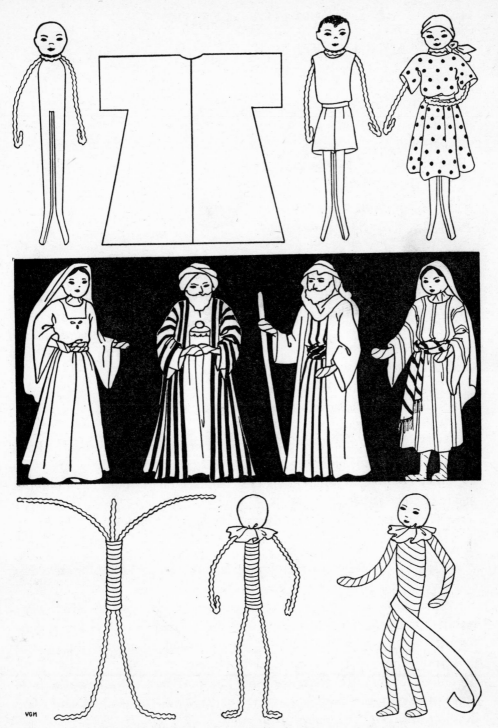

Clothespin and pipe cleaner figures for miniature scene

PIPE-CLEANER FIGURES

Materials

    Pipe cleaners.
    Heavy thread.
    Needles.
    Colored crepe paper.
    Cotton batting.
    Paste.

Procedure

Bind three pieces of pipe cleaner together. (See diagram on page 75.)

Cut circle of light orange crepe paper and stuff for head.

Fit head over the neck and tie on securely. Fit what is left over across the shoulders to fill them out.

Cut strips of light orange crepe paper about three eighths of an inch wide. Bend arms to the desired position and then wind with strips of light orange crepe paper to the desired thickness.

Do the same for the body and legs.

Wind bits of paper around ends of legs and turn up for feet.

Paint in the features.

Make hair by unraveling thick cotton embroidery threads of suitable color and sew onto the head.

The clothing depends upon the character of the doll and should be made of crepe paper.

These figures may be bent to assume natural positions. Standards may be made to hold them up or they may be suspended into the right positions on black threads.

Animals may also be made of pipe cleaners wound with crepe paper, or padded with cotton batting.

MODELED FIGURES

People and animals may be modeled with any of the modeling materials mentioned on pages 91 to 95.

SMALL DOLLS

Small dolls may be dressed to represent various characters.

MINIATURE ANIMALS AND BIRDS

With people collecting different kinds of miniature animals and birds it is often possible to get some of these to use in making dioramas. They may be introduced in the scene itself or they may serve as models for the children to look at when making their own figures. Encourage the children to get ideas from these miniatures but not to try to make exact copies.

SETTING THE SCENE

In arranging the diorama or scene care must be taken to follow certain rules, which will make all the difference between order and confusion.

The Rules

Each scene should tell a story or express a unified mood.

The most important part of the scene forms a center of interest and should be a little off center and toward the foreground of the scene.

The figures in this center of interest should be a trifle larger, or brighter, or more strikingly defined than less important figures.

To show perspective have near objects larger than those far away.

If less important figures look toward the center of interest it will lead the eye of the observer in that direction.

Balance the scene by having figures of equal importance opposite each other.

Backgrounds count as part of the picture, but they should be kept simple. Otherwise the background will detract from the center of interest.

A MINIATURE FARM SCENE

Materials

1. Heavy brown wrapping paper and colored construction paper.
2. Red, yellow, and orange crepe paper.
3. Straw or hay.
4. Cornstarch modeling material. (See page 91.)
5. Large piece of white wrapping paper for background.
6. Twigs about nine inches tall, which have many smaller twigs growing out of them.
7. Glue.
8. Crayons.

This scene may be built on a table, in a sand box, in a suitbox top, or on the shelf of a bookcase. One primary superintendent secured an old-fashioned china closet for her department, and this makes an excellent display cabinet.

Help the children to block out a forest of trees for the background. The drawing of these trees may be turned over to children who are particularly good at drawing. Other children may cut and fold house, barn, and chicken coop, using the 16-part square as a foundation. The shape may be varied by using an oblong instead of a square. These should be made of the heavy wrapping paper. Green roofs may be cut from the construction paper and pasted over the buildings, adding a more finished touch. Blinds should also be cut from the green paper and pasted in place.

Cut confetti of red, yellow, and orange crepe paper, mixing the colors well. Using a match put little dabs of glue on the twigs. While the glue is

A variety of buildings are made on a sixteen-square foundation

wet dip the twigs into the confetti. This makes attractive autumn trees. Push the stem of the twig into a lump of the modeling material, and press down flat on the table. This will make a good standard for the tree. By the following week it will be dry, then it can be painted brown to match the tree trunk. If the tree is still top-heavy, it is possible to put glue on the bottom of the standard, sticking it securely to the large piece of wrapping paper laid down for the foundation of the scene.

Apple trees may be made with red and green confetti.

Fruit and vegetables may be modeled out of the cornstarch material and painted bright colors. A roadside stand may be added if desired.

Farm animals should also be modeled. People may be made of pipe cleaners or of clothespins.

Individual groups will think of additional things to make the scene more realistic or interesting.

If the group likes to write, a series of stories may be written about the people who live on the farm, and what God does for them in the autumn. Bible verses may be chosen to use with the scene. The children may make a booklet with stories, pictures, and Bible material, or this material may be worked out on separate pieces of paper and later arranged on the bulletin board.

In the child's interest in making the scene and the book, be careful to keep the purpose of the unit in his mind. We are trying to show the beauty of God's world about us and to appreciate it more deeply as we see more and more evidences of his love and care.

THE PAPER CRÈCHE

Materials

1. Pictures to study or patterns to trace.
2. Heavy white drawing paper.
3. Tracing paper if the figures are to be traced.
4. Colored pencils, crayons, or paints, depending on the age and experience of the artists.
5. Cardboard for mounting.
6. Scissors.
7. Glue.
8. Carbon paper.

Freehand drawing of the figures is the creative way of making these figures though tracing is possible.

Trace the figures on the tracing paper and transfer the design to drawing paper, using the carbon paper or blackening the back of the tracing paper to make a carbon paper of it.

Color the figure, with due regard to the rules for color usage on the color chart; also study the use of color in famous paintings of the Madonna.

Glue this to the cardboard, taking care to spread the glue or paste thinly and evenly. Allow this to dry under a pile of magazines. This will insure smoothness. When it is perfectly dry (i.e. the next Sunday), cut the figures out. Glue them to standards made of little blocks of wood or to empty spools. These may then be arranged by the children to make an attractive tableau.

A stable may be made of heavy wrapping paper folded into sixteen squares. (See house pattern page 78.) Have the children make a thatched roof by cutting strips of yellow crepe-paper fringe and pasting it in overhanging layers. One side of the stable should be cut away so that some of the figures may be arranged inside.

Trees may be made according to the plan given for making palm trees on page 85.

Let the children experiment with arranging and rearranging the figures, giving each child a turn at this. Let them study famous paintings for arrangements.

THE PLYWOOD CRÈCHE. This kind of crèche is made much like the one above, but it is work better suited to junior boys.

Materials

1. Thin plywood.
2. Jig saw.
3. Sandpaper.
4. Tracing paper.
5. Crayons, colored pencils, paints, enamel or tempera.
6. Shellac.
7. Pattern.

Ideally the figures should be drawn freehand, on drawing paper and then transferred to the plywood. Cut them out with a jig saw. Sandpaper edges. If paints are used it is a help to score all lines with a jacknife. This helps to keep the colors from running together. When they are dry, shellac them. Small blocks of wood or spools may be glued onto the backs to make them stand up, or standards may be made of the salt and cornstarch mixture mentioned on page 91. The figures should be pressed into these standards while they are soft. The standards should be painted with water color while they are still moist.

This kind of crèche takes time. It could be started in church and taken home for the cutting and sandpapering if there are no facilities for such work at the church or if time is limited.

A wooden box might be used for the stable. This should have a hay roof and a window should be cut out at the back. Rough beams may be painted inside.

THE MODELED CRÈCHE. Charming figures have been modeled of plasticine, salt and cornstarch modeling material, or of clay by primary children. Of these materials plasticine is the easiest to handle if one is satisfied with temporary results. It can be used over and over again. Clay is the most durable and has the best texture, but it is fairly expensive, difficult to keep ready for use, and not easy to handle. If one has time and interested juniors, the results will justify the trouble.

A receipt for making the cornstarch and salt mixture is found on page 91. If this is well made and thoroughly mixed it makes a satisfactory modeling material which will take either water color or water-color pencil coloring well.

Materials

1. Plasticine, clay, or cornstarch and salt mixture.
2. Orange stick, match stick, or toothpicks for modeling tool.
3. Paper towels.
4. Oilcloth mats.
5. Paints or water-color pencils.
6. Little figures of Mary, Joseph, sheep, camels, etc., from dime store.

Let the children feel the articles from the dime store. It will give them a much better idea of what they hope to accomplish than looking at pictures. Discuss the various attitudes of the figures, asking such questions as, "Where is Mary looking? What is the Wise Man carrying?"

Tell the children to make a ball of their material first and then a fat roll of it. Show them how to pinch and poke it into position. Warn them to model the head as a part of the body and not separately.

Often the first lesson of this type may seem a failure, but the children are experimenting with a new medium and they are getting the feel of it. Skill will come with practice. Children usually like this type of work very much and will enjoy coming early and working on figures if it is done in the pre-session.

These figures should be kept very simple; their charm lies in attitude, not face. Almost no attempt at modeling faces should be made.

THE CLOTHESPIN CRÈCHE

Materials

1. Clothespins.
2. Salt and cornstarch modeling material.
3. Pipe cleaners.
4. Pieces of bright-colored silk for the Wise Men's clothing, brown cotton for shepherds, blue and rose color for Mary, white or pastel colors for angels, brown for Joseph, bits of striped cloth for turbans.
5. Colored crepe paper is an alternate suggestion.

See page 74 for instructions how to make clothespin dolls.

Using a jig saw you can cut off the end of a clothespin two inches from the top, to represent the baby, which should be wrapped in bands of white cloth. By bending Mary's arms she can be made to hold him.

Standards for these figures may be made of modeling material. The robes and dresses should be made long enough to hide the standard.

Use the three-section background described on page 70. This may be covered with plain dark-blue crepe paper, or it may have slip covers of wrapping paper on which is drawn the inside of a stable.

THE PAPIER-MÂCHÉ CRÈCHE. Another type of modeled crèche may be made out of papier-mâché. (See page 93.)

THE PEEP SHOW. The peep show is a miniature scene built at one end of a long box. At the other end is a hole through which the children can view the scene, which must be lighted from overhead.

Peep show of Chinese street scene

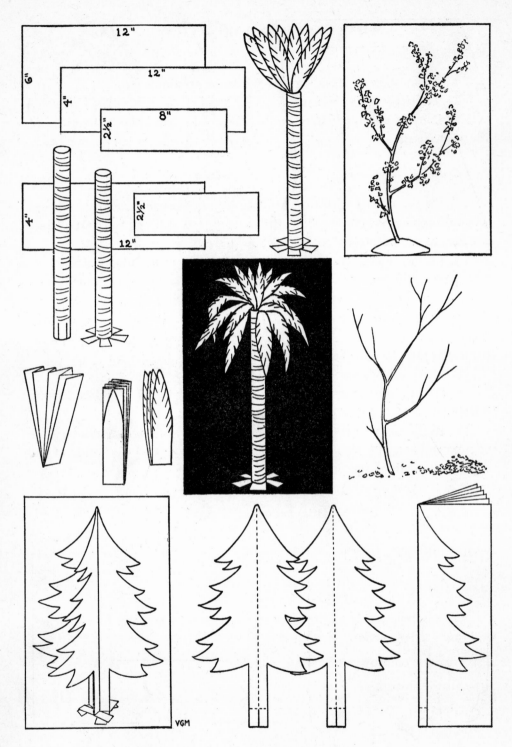

Palm trees, fruit trees or pine trees are used in miniature scenes

Materials

1. A shoe box or a box in which flowers are delivered.

2. Transparent cellophane.

3. Cardboard, crepe paper and whatever else is needed in building up the scene itself.

Procedure

1. Plan the scene with the children, deciding what materials are necessary to complete it and where the different objects will be placed. Introduce the idea of the peep show to them if they have never made one.

2. Collect all material necessary and have it ready to work with.

3. Set different children to work on the parts to be assembled later. Figures may be made of plywood, paper, or modeling material.

4. Arrange the objects which the children have made in the desired positions at one end of the box. By placing the largest figures toward the front you give the illusion of depth.

5. Make an interesting background.

6. At the other end of the box cut a peep hole 3 x 2 inches, pasting cellophane over the hole on the inside.

7. In the cover of the box at the end over the scene cut an oblong large enough to cover the scene, for illumination. Over this on the inside of the cover paste cellophane.

How to Make Trees

PALM TREES

Materials

Green crepe paper. (Three pieces, one 12 x 6 inches, one 12 x 4 inches, and one 8 x 2½ inches.)

Heavy wrapping paper (12 x 4 inches).

Brown crayon.

Glue.

Scissors.

Procedure

1. Make tube twelve inches high and one half inch in diameter. (Size can be varied according to size of the miniature scene.)

2. Color outside of tube a darker brown, taking care that the crayon marks go round and round the tube, for this adds to the illusion of roundness.

3. From base of tube cut up three fourths of an inch in several places and fold back these tabs which later will be used to make the tree stand.

4. Fold green crepe paper fanwise, having folds about an inch and a half apart. (See diagram on page 84.)

5. Cut leaf pattern, taking care that the leaves remain in a strip and are not cut apart. Fringe leaves according to the diagram.

6. Arrange leaves in a bunch with the small ones in the middle and tie with a string or thread.

7. Paste inside the tube at the top and insert the bunch of leaves.

8. Bend the leaves back to hang like palm leaves.

9. If wallboard is used for the base of the scene thumbtack the tree to base in desired position. Otherwise glue in place.

APPLE OR MAPLE TREES

Materials

Twigs shaped like small trees.
Orange, red, yellow, and brown crepe paper for autumn trees.
Green and red or pink crepe paper, according to season, for apple trees.
A tube of glue.
Spools of modeling material for base.

Procedure

1. After deciding what kind of tree you want cut several handfuls of the right-colored paper into confetti.

2. Put dabs of glue along the stems of the twigs and dip them into the confetti, which will stick to them and give the appearance of little trees with red and orange autumn foliage, or trees with pink apple blossoms or red fruit.

3. Either insert stems in spools and glue in place, or make bases for the trees, using the salt modeling mixture.

SIMPLE PINE TREES FOR LITTLE CHILDREN

Materials

Two pieces of green construction paper, or heavy wrapping paper to be colored with crayon.

Procedure

Put both papers together.

Fold vertically.

Draw half of a pine tree, making sure the fold comes where the middle of the tree comes. Have a flat base.

Cut this out.

You now have two trees exactly alike, each with a fold down the middle. Paste one half of one tree to one half of the other, and bend sides to make the tree stand up. (See diagram on page 84.)

OTHER PINE TREES

In rural communities or where it is possible to get Christmas tree branches, charming little trees may be made by inserting princess pine, ground pine, or bits of evergreen branches into spools which are colored brown if they are to be used as scenery or bright red if they are to be used for Christmas favors.

BABY CHRISTMAS TREES

Materials and Procedure

1. Princess pine, or pieces cut from lower branches of Christmas trees. These should be about four inches tall.
2. Empty spools.
3. Odd colored beads, as large and brightly colored as possible.
4. Thread.
5. Gay bits of Christmas wrapping paper.
6. Paste.

Tie the beads to the branches of the pine, clipping threads close so they will not show. Paste a strip of the fancy wrapping paper around the spool, choosing the brightest colors possible. Paste a circle of the wrapping paper over the top of the spool. Push the stem of the pine into the top of

Costumes for paper dolls correspond to the interests of the group

the spool, pushing bits of paper in around it to hold the tree upright. These can be mounted on a piece of cardboard and used as place cards. Baby Christmas trees may be a child's contribution to family table decoration, or they may be sent to the hospital for use as tray cards.

PAPER DOLLS

STORIES of children from other lands are made more real if the children make paper dolls to represent them. Let them study a costume before trying to reproduce it. This helps to fix it in their minds.

The finished dolls may be used in a number of ways. One of these is to have each child in the class make a different character from a story. When the dolls are finished, the table is cleared and the children use it for a stage, moving their characters about on the table and speaking their parts. Where real dramatization is impossible this makes a good substitute activity.

A stick about a foot long may be fastened to the back of a paper doll which then may be moved along the edge of the table and manipulated from below.

Sometimes the paper dolls are used in the little scenes which the children build up in sandboxes, suitbox tops, or on shelves in the bookcase. Sometimes they are pasted into the class book. Sometimes they are carried home to amuse a smaller child in the family. They should have some mission in life and be created with a definite aim in view.

Materials and Procedure

1. Paper-doll patterns. (The dime stores have books of paper dolls. Choose those most closely resembling real people. It is easier to make clothing for the dolls if their arms are held away from their bodies.)
2. White or tan drawing paper.
3. Colored pencils for younger children.
4. Water-color paints or colored pencils for older ones.
5. Scissors.
6. Colored construction paper or wall paper from sample books.

Show the children how to trace around the pattern. Put in hair line, chin line, and a few suggestions for underwear. Then have the children practice drawing faces on scrap paper. Make sure that the eyes are in the right position. Let them look at pictures of children's faces in books with

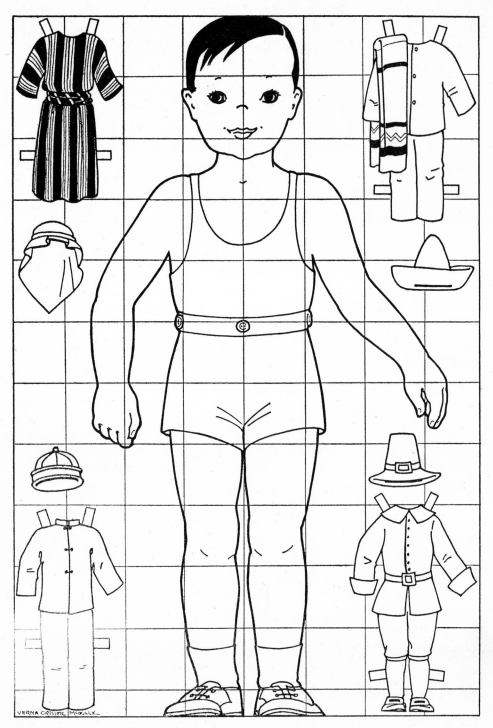

Story-book people come to life when represented by paper dolls

line drawings for illustrations. Encourage the children to make expressive faces by using only a few simple lines.

When the dolls are drawn they may be colored. For painting faces use a very light orange for the best effect.

The next step is dressing the dolls. Patterns should be used for this. The teacher lays the doll on paper and draws the pattern of dress or suit around it. Later she may teach the class to make patterns for their own characters.

When coloring the clothes, teach the children that certain colors blend more happily than others.

MODELING

THERE ARE many prepared clays on the market. Some are expensive, others crumble, and some are plastic and so cannot be used for anything permanent. The following rule for making a modeling substance is inexpensive and satisfactory.

1 cup salt	1 cup water
1 cup cornstarch	

Mix the above ingredients in the top of a double boiler and cook until the material forms a thick lump about the spoon. Stir constantly. Remove from stove and cool until it can be handled. Dust your hands with cornstarch and knead the mixture until it is smooth and of even texture; then roll it in a ball and wrap in oiled paper. Keep in an airtight box; exposure to air dries and hardens it. This material will keep plastic several weeks if it is properly taken care of and is particularly useful in making the Christmas crèche, scenes from foreign lands, and Bible scenes. It is much cleaner to use than many of the prepared clays.

The modeled figures should be allowed to dry. Then they can be painted with water color or colored with crayon.

STUCCO. While the above material is useful for modeling, stucco is better for spreading, particularly for making Oriental houses, and attractive maps showing mountains and valleys.

1 cup flour	Enough water to make the consistency
1 cup salt	of thick frosting

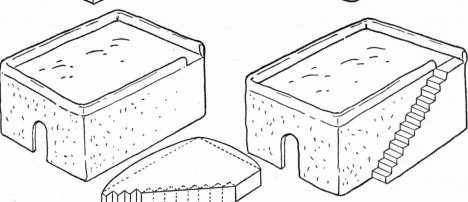

Stucco house for Palestinian scenes

Mix together until smooth. This material may be spread over the cardboard models of houses or on maps. When dried it may be painted with water color.

It is well to have the tables covered with a piece of oilcloth and to have the children's clothing protected by oilcloth aprons. These can be made in one of the handwork classes.

This stucco is spread on with a knife. In making the Oriental house one can either cover an inverted cardboard box with stucco or make a box of cardboard. The first is the easier method. Cut out an arched doorway. Spread the stucco evenly first on the sides and then on the top. To make this even and smooth dip a knife in warm water and run it lightly over the surface. Then let the house dry. This will take several days.

The following Sunday model a railing to put on the top and stairs for the side. These should be made out of the cornstarch and salt modeling material described above, for one cannot model with stucco. Pat some of this material out flat, and cut out a flight of stairs. A bit of glue on the back of these will stick them onto the house. The railing may be modeled on, using the fingers.

This stucco may also be used in making an Eskimo scene. A large old rubber ball may be cut in two and each half covered with stucco to make igloos. Icebergs may be cut from pieces of cardboard and covered with a blue-green stucco.

To make colored stucco, tempera or colored ink may be mixed into the stucco before it is spread or painted on after it is dry.

PAPER PULP. Paper pulp is useful in modeling relief maps or for making the heads of fist puppets.

Materials

The clean edges of newspapers, without any printing on them.
Boiling water.

Procedure

Cut the edges from old newspapers and cut them into small pieces.
Pour boiling water over them. Use as much as they will absorb.
Let stand several hours.
Stir till your modeling material is a softened mass and the pieces of paper lose all their original shape.
Add water or drain off water until the mixture seems a good consistency for modeling.
After this has been worked into figures and is dried out it may be painted.
See Fist Puppets. (Page 99.)

PAPIER-MÂCHÉ. This is an excellent modeling material, and lends itself to the making of many interesting things. It is especially good for making objects and people for the miniature scene, the Christmas crèche, heads and hands for fist puppets, built-up scenery for dioramas, and houses. The materials needed are inexpensive and easy to obtain, and results are usually satisfactory.

Papier-mâché requires care in handling, and keen observation. It is sticky, so tables and clothes should be protected.

Procedure for making papier-mâché figure of Wise Man

Materials

> Paper towels or newspaper or paper pulp.
> Tissue paper.
> Liquid paste.

Procedure

1. Discuss problem with the child. He should know what he is making, about how large it will be, and its general shape.

2. Cut strips about three eighths of an inch wide from paper towels.

3. Make a core, roughly the shape of the object to be modeled, using dampened paper towels or paper pulp.

4. Brush paste on core.

5. Dampen strips of paper towel and bind them about core to hold it in shape. Dampening the strips helps them to go on smoothly. Completely cover the core with strips, making sure that they adhere firmly.

6. After the core is covered, begin to fill in places where more bulk is desirable. Keep adding strips dipped in paste or laid against a sticky core till there are several layers of paper and paste. The paste not only fastens the strips in place, but it also helps the figure to harden. Small pieces may be fastened in place to build up the contours of nose, lips, cheeks, and forehead of puppets, and ears of animals.

7. When this rough foundation has been formed as well as possible the finishing touches are put on. The whole surface of the object is brushed with paste, and several layers of damp tissue paper are smoothed on. Be careful that this paper is put on without wrinkles. If plenty of paste is used and the paper is smoothed gently into place with a pencil this is not too difficult.

8. The object is then put aside to dry.

9. When it is dry it may be painted with poster paint.

10. A coat of shellac over the painted surface will protect the paint and help harden the figure.

Papier-mâché can also be made by mixing sawdust and paste together until stiff enough to use as a modeling material.

This activity is better for juniors than for primary children. The work may be carried on at odd times, because it can be left at a minute's notice without harm, and resumed later.

A moving picture, "Living with the Migrants"

The Moving Picture

MAKING A "MOVIE" is an activity which has many uses and can be adapted to many situations. Bible stories, stories of world friendship, life in other lands, and the work done by missionaries at home and abroad may all be depicted in this fashion. It is a piece of work which will occupy the efforts of as many children as there are in the group, which makes it a co-operative undertaking.

The moving picture itself is a series of pictures on a long strip of paper or curtain cloth which is wound from one roller to another. These rollers are attached to the sides of a box, preferably made of wood, which is the theater.

Materials

1. A fairly large wooden or corrugated paper box.
2. Rollers cut from an old broomstick. These should be a little taller than the box.
3. A long strip of heavy brown wrapping paper or, still better, curtain shade cloth. A little less in width than the height of the box.
4. Cardboard or thin plywood for proscenium arch to be placed as a frame around opening of box if desired. This should be about two inches longer and three inches higher than the opening of the box.
5. Colored pencils, crayons, or poster paints.
6. Glue or thumbtacks with which to fasten paper to rollers.
7. Four small blocks of plywood to hold front from box thus providing a slot through which the paper may be rolled.

Procedure

Start with a story. When the story has been told to the children they should discuss it and break it up into scenes. Each child chooses or is assigned a scene to illustrate, with colored crayons, pencils, or whatever medium is desired. This should be done on scrap paper at first of the size desired for the finished work in the moving picture. Sometimes a group makes individual pictures which are pasted in the correct order on the strip. A more satisfactory method when there are fewer children is to divide the strip and work directly on it; the only disadvantage in this method being that only one child at a time can work on it.

Fist puppet with head made from ball of darning cotton

The work should be divided in such a way that each child has a part assigned to him and is responsible for it. One child might make the cardboard front, another paint the theater box, while a third glues the blocks to the corners of the box itself. The proscenium arch is then glued to the blocks. After the pictures have been drawn on the strip captions may be composed by the children and written under each picture. Or captions may be written in spaces between the pictures.

When the strip is ready it is threaded between the front and the theater box. The ends of the strip are then thumbtacked or glued to the rollers and rolled into place. Loops may be fastened around ends of rollers to hold rollers and script in position. If the front of the theater is wider and higher than the opening of the box the roller mechanism will be hidden from the public.

For sound effects children can speak for the characters as the pictures unroll. The writing of the dialogue is a still different type of creative activity. This activity is better suited to juniors than to primary children though an upper primary group will be able to get satisfactory results with help in the mechanism.

Fist Puppets

Fist Puppets, or mitten puppets as they are sometimes called, are little manikins made to wear over the hand. These may take the shapes of both people and animals. There are several ways of making heads, but they must always be very light weight for easier manipulation of the puppet.

These puppets may be used in dramatization either with or without a frame theater. It is remarkable to see how they come to life once a child's hand is in them, and what lovable creations they can be to their owners. Characters from Bible and other stories can be made, as well as world-friendship puppets. One of the simplest may be made as follows:

Materials

1. A medium-sized ball of darning cotton.
2. An eight-inch square of flesh-colored cloth.
3. Yarn for hair and beard if necessary.
4. Suitable cloth for garments.
5. Elastic bands.

6. Embroidery silks.

7. Cardboard for the neck core and hands.

8. For animals, velvet or woolen cloth can be used. Fur fabric is even better.

Procedure

Roll a piece of cardboard 2½ x 4 inches into a tube and glue it. Slip this into one end of the darning-cotton ball. Cover the ball with the flesh-colored cloth, holding it in place with an elastic band at the neck and pulling the cloth as smooth as possible. Do not cut off any of the surplus cloth because it will help to fill out the clothing. Embroider the features onto the face, taking care that the eyes are halfway down the ball. Arrange the hair according to the character of the doll and sew into place. The children should study pictures of the character they are trying to make to determine the features and kind of hair.

The clothing depends upon the character also, but a universal foundation garment is necessary. This is cut kimono style and should be large enough to cover the hand and forearm comfortably. (See diagram on opposite page.) The hands are made of cardboard and sewed into the sleeve. Outer garments may be made to suit the character portrayed.

When making animals the procedure is much the same except that the foundation garment is made of the velvet or furry cloth. Instead of hands, sew the ends of the sleeves together. The head depends upon the animal portrayed. The darning ball can be used for a round-headed animal such as a cat. To make horses and dogs a profile, such as is shown in stuffed animals, should be drawn. After the cardboard core is inserted in the neck the rest of the head is stuffed with cotton. Buttons make good eyes and yarn may be used for manes. Ears of whatever material seems suitable may be added.

This type of activity is better suited to juniors and to the midweek period, and the puppets may be sent home for stitching and sewing.

FIST PUPPETS IN PAPIER-MÂCHÉ. The heads and hands of fist puppets may also be made of papier-mâché. (See page 93 for general explanation.)

Model the core, which should be about the size of a golf ball, pressed into an egg shape, over your forefinger so there will be a hole in the finished head for the finger that animates it. The neck should be modeled around a tube of stiff paper pressed around your finger.

Fist puppet with papier-mâché head and hands

If the features are exaggerated they will be more interesting when the puppet is made to move, and these should be painted with stronger than natural colors.

Costume these dolls according to character, but have a kimono foundation such as is shown on page 98.

SLIDES FOR THE STEREOPTICON PROJECTOR

WITH VISUAL EDUCATION taking its proper place as a teaching method, projectors are being used more and more. Whereas it is possible to buy or rent slides at not too great cost, there is great educational value in making them as well. This work is not too difficult, and it will give great satisfaction to the children. Slides can be made by older primary pupils though the work is more adapted to juniors. It is a particularly satisfying medium to those who are naturally artistic.

The possibilities of making and using slides is endless. One class may be studying the story of Joseph. They have studied pictures illustrating his adventures, and have traced his journey on the map. They may decide that they would like to share their information with the entire department. Then they agree that one very interesting way to do this would be to have slides and a script to go with them.

There is more planning which finally results in a working outline similar to the following:

1. Joseph's boyhood
   a. His early travels
      (picture of a caravan of camels, donkeys, herds)
   b. The tent home
   c. The coat of many colors
   d. Joseph sold
   e. Map showing his travels
2. Joseph in Egypt
   a. In his master's house
   b. Joseph in prison
   c. In the king's palace
3. The Famine
   a. The dream
   b. Joseph's plan
   c. Years of plenty
   d. The drought
4. Joseph and his brothers
   a. The brothers come before him
   b. The accusation that they were spies and the demand for Benjamin
   c. The money in the bags
   d. The brothers and their father
   e. Benjamin in Egypt
   f. The silver cup
   g. Judah's offer
   h. Joseph's revelation
   i. Joseph and his father

Then the class assigns the work of drawing the pictures for the slides and writing the script, half the class writing script, the other half drawing pictures, or each child may be assigned a picture and the script that describes it.

Another group may be working on a world friendship project. They may be enjoying the adventures of a migrant family in the Far West. They may decide to illustrate the story with slides as a climax to their project to send gifts to a migrant center, or they may decide to make up a story of their own and illustrate it with slides.

Another group may be working on a church project, learning about the symbols of the church. These can be reproduced for slides.

Slides may be made interpreting hymns, such as "America the Beautiful," "For the Beauty of the Earth," "Come, Ye Thankful People, Come," or any other with pictorial suggestion and used effectively in a service of worship.

There are many Bible verses which suggest pictures and which may be illustrated. "I was glad when they said unto me, let us go into the house of the Lord." "This is the Lord's doing; it is marvelous in our eyes." "He hath made everything beautiful in its time." "The Lord is good." "Your Heavenly Father feedeth them."

Many possibilities will suggest themselves to the teacher who is truly interested in carrying out such types of handwork. Now let us look at methods.

SILHOUETTE SLIDES

Materials

1. Pieces of clear cellophane 3¼ by 4 inches.
2. Black silhouette paper.
3. Scissors.
4. Two pieces of glass 3¼ by 4 inches.
5. Passe partout.
6. Adhesive tape.

These slides are made by cutting out silhouettes of people, trees, animals, etc., which the picture requires, and pasting them onto the cellophane. The cutting can be done freehand or pictures can be drawn first and then cut out. Show the children that the secret of a good silhouette is in choosing figures with decided and characteristic outlines. The arranging and glueing is fussy and particular work. The teacher should experiment by making a

MALTESE CROSS

CELTIC CROSS

CROSS FLEURIE

TRIANGLE

TREFOIL

TREFOIL AND
THREE POINTS

TRIQUETRA

Silhouettes of Christian symbols

slide before she tries to teach a class to do it. In this way she anticipates difficulties and knows how to meet them. (See page 32.)

A little glass folder should be made to hold the slide before the light. Bind the two pieces of glass around the edges with the passe partout. Then fasten them together on one side with adhesive tape. This makes a little booklet into which the slide may be slipped, and which may be used over and over again with any number of slides.

A card catalogue with envelopes instead of cards makes a convenient and safe place in which to file slides. These may also be used profitably more than once.

INDIA INK AND CELLOPHANE SLIDES. Older children can make slides using India ink, transparent water colors, and cellophane.

Materials

1. Pieces of cellophane $3\frac{1}{4}$ by 4 inches.
2. India ink.
3. Transparent water colors.
4. Brushes with fine points.
5. Glass folder such as described above.

Children may lay their pieces of cellophane over a picture and trace it, using India ink and brush, or they may draw their own picture on drawing paper and trace it onto the cellophane. When the ink is perfectly dry the picture may be painted, using transparent water colors. These are put into the glass folders when finished, and may be filed in envelopes in a card catalogue.

GLASS SLIDES. The etched glass slide is easier for the smaller children to make and is recommended for the primary department.

Materials

1. Pieces of etched glass $3\frac{1}{4}$ by 4 inches.
2. Transparent indelible pencils.
3. Cellophane covers.
4. Passe partout.

Draw the picture with lead pencil. Color it with the transparent indelible pencil, taking pains to leave no spaces unevenly colored. A painted effect will be obtained by going over the color with a wet brush. Bright colors are better than dull ones. After the slide is colored, cover the drawing with a piece of transparent cellophane, binding it on with passe partout. This prevents the colors from running and smudging.

NATURE ACTIVITIES

FEEDING THE BIRDS. Children are interested in birds, and establishing bird feeding stations during the winter is a worth-while activity, both from the point of view of making the bird feeding stations and of the sustained interest created. A bird feeding station may be simple or elaborate, according to the age and ability of its builder.

A simple wooden box suspended from a limb of a tree makes a satisfactory feeder. Such a box should be about twelve inches in height and depth.

A narrower box may be fastened, facing outwards, on the window sill. A narrow piece of wood that will serve both as a perch and to keep food from spilling out should be fastened to the bottom of this box. One disadvantage of the window-sill box is that the bird guests cannot be seen from the house unless the back of the box is knocked out.

Chickadees, nuthatches, and woodpeckers are very fond of greasy foods. A doughnut swung from the top of the feeding station will prove a tempting repast for the little upside-down chickadee. Suet, bread spread with peanut butter, and bones with bits of meat clinging to them will tempt these birds. Juncoes like seed, and special mixtures for wild birds may be bought at stores selling seed and garden supplies. Breadcrumbs are well liked also.

Even if your bird guests are nothing but dusty little sparrow gamins from the street, the delight in seeing them feed and in feeling that they are becoming tame will be worth while. Caring for others, even if the others are only sparrows, is following the Golden Rule.

BIRD HOUSES. Most boys of junior age like to make bird houses. Various styles, both simple and elaborate, can be made. There is no accounting for the taste of birds. A beautiful pair of bluebirds, after carefully looking over a prize bird house, made a nest and reared a family in an opposite tree, in an old chalk box with a hole cut in it, much to the disgust of the boy who put up both houses.

Children who make bird baths and put up bird houses are engaged in projects of civic value, for birds are valuable in destroying many insect pests. In connection with this work it would be well to tell the story of the birds of Killingworth, adapted from a poem by Longfellow, and also the story of St. Francis and the birds. The children might also look up verses about birds in the Bible. A notebook could be kept, containing records of the raising of any bird families, also pictures of neighborhood birds, copies of bird poems, and the bird verses from the Bible.

Bird houses should be built, taking into consideration the requirements of hoped-for occupants. Many people, in building houses intended for wrens and bluebirds, make the mistake of cutting too large a hole for the door, thus inviting English sparrows. The door for these small birds should not be larger than a 25-cent piece. The simpler the house the more apt one is to get bird tenants, for birds are skeptical of elaborate homes. They like their houses to blend into the surroundings. For this reason, it is best to paint them either dark green or brown to resemble foliage or branches.

The use of houses made from tin cans is to be discouraged, for tin gets too hot in the sun. The government issues a very good pamphlet on bird houses and the attracting of birds to a locality, and these may be obtained by asking for them. Children should be cautioned against putting bird houses in places where cats can get at them easily. Bird houses should be attached securely. The best bird houses are built in such a way that they may be cleaned every spring.

In a fifth-grade group of about thirty-five children three fourths of the class made bird houses and over half of these held bird families by the middle of June. This activity is particularly good for the midweek session or for some extra session planned for this purpose. This is a junior activity.

THE BIRDS' CHRISTMAS TREE. A winter project of establishing a winter feeding station for the birds arouses much interest among the children. The fact that God uses the minds and hands of his people to carry out his work should be the underlying thought during the working out of this project.

Older children should be asked to study the matter of maintaining bird feeding stations from books at the library. They may write to the Department of Agriculture, Washington, D. C., for bulletins on attracting birds to various sections of the country and on bird feeding stations.

If there is an evergreen tree on the church grounds it may be used. If not, perhaps some child will donate a discarded Christmas tree.

Popcorn may be strung, pieces of suet tied on, stale doughnuts strung up and little paper cups filled with a mixture of melted suet and peanut butter tied in place. Once established, the feeding station should be maintained during the winter, and the responsibility of checking up on the food and replenishing it when needed should be taken seriously by both teacher and class.

THE NATURE MUSEUM. Making a nature museum may be either a fall or spring activity. Its purpose is to show examples of God's care and thought for his outdoor world. This is an excellent activity for the vacation school or camp.

The Museum

1. Orange box cases

Paint these first with a coat of flat white. Then paint them with green or brown, or cream-colored enamel. They may later be used as bookcases or files for materials belonging to various classes. Protect the children who are painting with aprons and the floor with newspapers.

2. Vases and containers for seed sprays

Glass jars of pleasing shapes may be painted with colored enamel or designs glued on and then shellac applied.

3. Screens

Use pieces of burlap, cambric, black cheesecloth or unbleached muslin. The size depends on the size of the space where it is to be hung. Make a two-inch hem at the top and bottom of the screen. Yardsticks may be put through these hems to keep the screen straight.

4. Frieze

See page 132. Subjects for frieze might include the life history of a toad, the cycle of a plant from one seed to many, or wonders in God's out-of-door world. It might be a series of autumn pictures showing God's provision for the winter.

5. Seed Charts

These should show various provisions made for seed dispersal.

6. Posters

Let these illustrate Bible verses concerning God's care.

7. Explanations

Children write several sentences about each object in their museum, explaining why they put it there and what it shows about God's plan. These may be on cards and laid near the exhibit.

8. Temporary cages for insects and small animals

The comfort of the occupant should be considered, and as soon as the exhibit is over, little wild things should be set free. The children should look up the proper diets for their creatures.

9. Decorated boxes for seed displays, shells, etc.

Cardboard boxes covered with wall paper, lined, and divided into compartments, or cigar boxes painted or decorated with paper.

10. Stained-glass windows.

See page 114. In making these for windows with small panes let each child design a pane, using some nature motif.

11. Oral Explanations

Have each child prepared to talk about some one part of the exhibit, telling how it helps reveal the mind of God at work.

12. Pictures

Children may draw pictures which illustrate the points they are demonstrating.

GRASSHOPPER AND CRICKET CAGE. (Primary or junior activity.)

Materials

1. Glass fish tank or bowl.
2. Piece of wire screen to cover the top.
3. Piece of sod with grass growing.
4. Food, such as petals of flowers, bread, apple.

The purpose of carrying out such an activity is to arouse an interest in God's little creatures, and a sense of responsibility in caring for them. In church school where daily care is impossible the little creatures should be released at the close of the period.

Two poems that would add to this discussion are "A Fairy Went a Marketing" and "Little People in the Grass." Both poems are in the collection, *Silver Pennies,* and both bring out the desirability of being kind to the "little people."

Cages can also be made of cardboard boxes and mosquito netting.

GARDEN ACTIVITIES. If all seeds dropped down under the parent plant there would be no room for them and not enough plant food in the ground to support them. Nature has provided some very interesting ways of scattering seeds from the mother plant, and the children should be taught to look behind the wonders of nature to their source.

One group was very interested in "The Garden's Treasure Boxes." Hollyhock "cookie boxes," poppy "pepper shakers" and other seed containers were brought in and discussed. Some of these were drawn. Others were blueprinted. Some were pinned on a screen, and others separated into little pill boxes. The children were much interested in the different sizes, shapes, and mechanisms for dispersal.

A. *Seed Chart.*

Materials

1. Large piece of wrapping paper divided into sixths, with the following heads:

a. Winged Adventurers	*d.* Treasure Boxes
b. Sailors	*e.* Bird Express
c. Hitchhikers	*f.* Fruit Seed

2. Seeds, pictures of seeds, etc.
3. Glue.
4. Scotch tape.

The seeds brought in by the children are glued or fastened to the proper section of the chart. Pictures of fruit may be used and a written account of each section should be included. Bible verses may be added.

B. *Seed Stories.*

Let the children pretend to be seeds and write stories telling of their adventures in being carried from the parent plant.

C. *Seed Prayers.*

Pretend a seed could thank God for his care and thoughtful planning. What might it say? (See Page 128.)

SEED EXPERIMENTS. Plant large seeds, such as nasturtiums, heavenly blue morning glories, lima beans, etc. Let children discuss what they need. Each child should have a few planted in a paper pot to take home. Let them report from week to week on the progress of their plants. Help them to recognize the miracle of a seed, and be grateful to God whose wisdom planned the workings of the universe.

These seed experiments should be written up in the class book with illustrations. A litany of thanksgiving and appreciation may be worked out with the children.

The little plants may be presented as gifts, or be planted in gardens or window boxes. Even crowded city houses have their bits of green in windows or in boxes on the roof.

Slipping Plants

A straggly old geranium or begonia plant will provide many slips and be all the better for drastic trimming. We may say, "God has wonderful plans for making sure that there will always be certain plants. We are going to find out about one of these today," or, "We are going to make an experiment with a geranium plant. Perhaps this experiment will show us something about God. Let us see if we can discover what it shows." In either case after the successful experiment we should go back to our original statement and carry it to a conclusion.

Materials

An old geranium or begonia plant.

Individual flowerpots. Paper ones can be used, or tin cans with holes punched in the bottoms are satisfactory.

Enough good soil for flowerpots.

A box of sand.

Water.

Newspapers to protect tables.

A large kitchen spoon.

Several jelly tumblers.

Pieces of broken flowerpot.

Procedure

1. Explain purpose of the experiment. Let children discuss what they would like to do with their little plants. This might include giving them to friends, sending them to a hospital, etc.

2. Let the children cut off small branches of the plant. These should be about four or five inches high. Show them how to nip off all buds and

Garden activities may include "slipping plants," making plant holders, and decorating seed envelopes

blossoms, explaining that by doing this the strength of the plant will go into making roots.

3. Let some plant their slips in wet sand and let others put theirs into glasses of water. Make arrangements to have someone water those in the sand at least once during the week. Explain that these are two ways of helping the plant put out new roots.

4. The following week, if roots have started, plant the slips in soil. Put a piece of flowerpot at the bottom of each container to provide drainage.

5. Let the children take their plants home. Tell them to keep them in the shade for several days and then put them in a sunny window.

6. Write the experiment in the class book, being sure to include the results of their thinking about God's plan.

7. Follow up from time to time. Keep a record of how many new plants came from one old one, and what was done with each small plant.

BULBS. Plant bulbs either in soil or in water or both, to give as gifts or to make the department beautiful.

Stress the fact that those planted in water had enough food stored in the bulb to make them grow and blossom. Here again children may see the mind of God at work.

PLANT HOLDERS. Plant holders are used to hold house plants erect. They may serve as gifts. Birds, butterflies, and conventional flower patterns may be used. The children should design these themselves and not trace them from other sources.

Materials

Bamboo sticks from twelve to eighteen inches long. (Seed companies sell these.)

Construction paper or thin plywood.

Poster paints or crayons.

Shellac for wooden holders.

Glue.

Procedure for Paper-topped Holders

Make design on trial paper first. (See butterfly on opposite page.)

Transfer it to light-colored construction paper.

Cut it out.
Transfer design to other side of the butterfly.
Color both sides.
Glue to the top of the stick.
Fold back wings.

Procedure for Wooden-topped Holders

This is a better activity for boys who have had some practice with jig saws.

Make design and transfer it to the wood.
Cut it out with a jig saw.
Transfer pattern to other side.
Paint both sides.
Shellac.
Fasten to the top of the stick either with small U-shaped nails or glue.

GARDEN MARKERS. Garden markers are used in a garden to mark rows of seeds before they come up. They may be made as gifts or for personal use.

Materials

Tongue depressers.
Wax crayons, wax pencils, or poster paint.

Procedure

Plan design for the marker on paper. A conventional design or naturalistic drawing of the plant which is to be marked can be used with the printed name of the plant. Transfer design onto marker. Color the design and then shellac it.

TRANSPARENCIES

STAINED-GLASS WINDOW TRANSPARENCY

Materials and Procedure

1. Black construction paper.
2. Colored cellophane or bright-colored tissue paper.
3. Glue or paste.
4. Newspaper for experimentation.

Using a plate for a pattern trace a circle onto the black construction paper. Each child will need two circles. This is for a rose window. A Gothic window can be made also, but it is more difficult to make a design to fill it up.

Now cut circles of newspaper for experimenting. Fold one of them into halves first, then fourths, and then eighths. Show children how to make a flower center. Open the circle up. Is it too large? Too small? Try again if the first one was not satisfactory. When a child does make a good one let him fold both black papers together and cut out a similar center.

Experiment yourself beforehand so you will know what the difficulties are. Warn the children when they cut into a fold, not to cut through to the other side or the design will not come out whole.

When a lacy design is completed take the two pieces of black and separate them. Then decide which colors go happily together. Cut pieces of the tissue or cellophane to paste over the holes of the design, remembering to balance the colors. A thin sheet of white paper which allows light through pasted over the entire surface will give an opaque window which is more satisfactory than the transparent one. When all the bits of colored paper are pasted into place paste the second black design over the first, taking care that all parts of the design correspond. Lay a newspaper over the transparency and then pile books or magazines on it in order that it may dry flat.

When the transparencies are completed they may be fastened to the windows, using pieces of Scotch tape to hold them in place, or they may be taken home.

CHRISTMAS TRANSPARENCIES

Materials

1. Black construction paper.
2. Medium blue tissue paper.
3. Paste.
4. Scissors.
5. Pictures or patterns.

A whole series of Christmas transparencies were made by a fifth-grade group. These were cut out of black paper and mounted on blue tissue paper, and represented four, large, plain glass windows, each window divided into two sections. The tissue paper was cut to fill up the space and was about eighteen inches high.

Some of the figures used were copied from patterns in books although they had to be enlarged to be effective. Others were cut freehand, while others were drawn and cut out afterward. The figures of persons were about seven or eight inches tall.

One scene represented the canopy type of stable. In the center was the child, with Mary kneeling by him. The other figures were of Joseph and the shepherd with two lambs.

Another scene showed just a church crowning a hill, with two little pines on either side.

Still another represented the Wise Men on their camels, coming from the East.

Another was of three Scandinavian children erecting a large bundle of grain for the birds. Several birds were in the sky.

Shepherds in the fields watching over their flocks made another scene.

English children bringing in the yule log and children around a Christmas tree were others.

A wise teacher keeps a file of Christmas cards which can be used for ideas.

WORSHIP CENTERS

WORSHIP CENTERS are arranged to create atmosphere and to help children reach a worshipful frame of mind. They should be carefully planned. Too often the leader does all the planning and arranging. Considerable educational values in religion would be derived from presenting the problem to the department and then turning it over to various classes as class assignments.

The leader should present the problem early in the year by discussing the following questions with the group:—

1. What is a worship center?
2. Why do churches and church schools have them?
3. What kind of feeling should they suggest?
4. What objects are used to make a worship center truly worshipful?
5. What must we guard against?

Show pictures of worship centers in other churches and comment upon them. Let the children tell what they liked about them. Let them describe worship centers they would like to arrange.

Procedure for making stained-glass window transparency

If the following points were not brought out in the discussion, present them:—

1. A worship center should be kept simple and restful. It should not distract the mind from worship, but be in harmony with it, as we hope its use will lead to quiet, thoughtful meditation.

2. It should be in keeping with the service planned by the leader, or with the season of year. Groups should confer with the leader to find the theme of the worship service, in order that there may be a relationship between service and center.

3. Arrangements should be varied. Using the same objects in the same way each Sunday is not creative. Interest is lost, and the center will be a routine affair. Variety will awaken interest, comment, and feeling.

4. The worship center should always be beautiful. The children will learn something of the joy of creating lovely flower arrangements and of working with the beautiful. They should be taught that it is their responsibility to make their part of the church as beautiful as possible.

5. The center may represent service. Occasionally money from the children's benevolence fund may be voted for church-school flowers or for a plant to be used as a part of the worship center and then sent to a sick member of the school, or someone else who is ill or who needs a bit of cheer.

6. The objects used should help turn thoughts toward God as the creator of loveliness, master artist, and giver of all good gifts.

OBJECTS

The Bible—A large family Bible of past years is excellent to use, as its size and beauty command respect, but any Bible can be used.

Candles—Candles suggest illumination. Some children do understand and love symbolism, and can be taught to appreciate it more. Helping them to understand symbolism will help them to interpret the symbols of the church.

Flowers—Garden flowers in season should be used. Help the children to know the joy of sharing their gardens with others. Wild flowers also should be used, for children should be taught to see beauty in their form and color and to recognize it as a part of God's plan. Arranging these may be a happy creative experience. Plants make beautiful arrangements.

The Cross—Many use the cross as a focal point. The cross is particularly appropriate at Easter and little else should be used with it. Making a cross might be the problem of a class of boys. Simple beautiful ones may be made of slender white birch trunks, cut to the right proportion. With ferns and simple wild flowers against a blue background, lovely effects may be produced.

The Cover—Usually there is but one cover for the worship center. It may be light brown, blue, purple, or green. It might be well to have several covers of different colors made to harmonize with the seasons or holidays. Tan makes a lovely neutral background for flaming autumn leaves or brilliant fall flowers. Blue might be the base of the Christmas crèche. Purple is appropriate for Easter.

Pictures—Each department should have many pictures, and some of these should be large enough and lovely enough for the worship center. It is well to have a simple frame with a movable back so that pictures can be changed at will. A few rules for choosing and displaying pictures follow.

1. Use only one at a time; more distract and divide the attention.

2. Choose pictures in the spirit of worship; quiet ones that do not tell a story to excite the imagination. Millet's "Angelus" and "Song of the Lark" are good examples. Madonnas and pictures of the head of Christ are also in keeping. Children should be taught the importance of making good choices.

3. Vary the selection, considering the theme of the service, the time of year, and the spirit of worship.

4. Use pictures large enough to be plainly seen.

5. Place pictures at about eye level, either behind the table or on it. A simple easel may be made to hold them.

The Offering Plate—Too often we are content to use the same offering plate or basket year after year. There should be one beautiful container at least—a wooden bowl or a pottery dish, but it should command respect. Value is derived from having children make or decorate containers. They might get an unpainted wooden bowl, design a decoration for it, transfer it into the bowl, paint it with poster paint and then shellac the whole thing. They might make a clay bowl.

The May offering might be taken in a beautiful May basket. One church school had a miniature church bank. A primary department that was collecting money to provide milk for poor children used a milk bottle to suggest the purpose of their gift.

Novelty containers may be used occasionally to create interest and arouse enthusiasm, but do have at least one beautiful container to use often in harmony with the spirit of worship.

Wall Hangings—Some worship centers need some sort of wall hanging for background. This may be a simple curtain, matching the cover of the table, upon which one lovely picture may be hung. One group spatter-printed a hanging, using a design of ferns and leaves. (See page 32.) Another cut silhouettes of the Christmas story and spatter-printed them on a lovely rich blue background. Still another group drew a map of Palestine on a large piece of unbleached muslin. They drew pictures upon it and colored it with crayon. This they ironed into the cloth. Then they embroidered around the edges and between the colors, using colored embroidery thread and the outline stitch. Charts, showing service activity, may sometimes be used as a background.

The Triptych—The triptych is like a three-part screen, the top of each part shaped in a Gothic arch, and the three parts hinged together. This may be a simple frame to be filled in with a stained-glass window (see page 29), or it may be made of wall board and used for pictures.

Creativity is combining known ingredients into new patterns. Give your pupils an opportunity to make their worship center truly their own by allowing them to choose, arrange, and vary. However, teach them the principles of good arrangement. Help them to be more thoughtful in their choice of ingredients, and show them their responsibility in making the church of God more beautiful.

A frieze of the Christmas story is drawn

BIBLE STORIES

ONE OF THE objectives of Christian education is increasing familiarity with the Bible and other related literature. There is a great difference between learning by head and learning by heart. To memorize simply for the sake of giving back the material verbatim does not accomplish the desired end. In teaching children we must choose material which can be translated into daily living and enrichment of the mind at the level of the child's understanding.

There is much in the Bible that can be understood even by little children. Often it is a complete beautiful thought expressed in a single verse. These should be stored up in a child's mind for present and later use so that when he becomes more familiar with his Bible and meets them it will be like coming to a familiar guidepost or meeting an old friend.

INTERPRETATION. The teacher provides pictures to illustrate the material he intends to use. The picture of a child helping someone in trouble might be used with the verse, "Be ye kind, one to another." (Eph. 4:32.) A series of pictures of the different seasons would illustrate, "He hath made everything beautiful in its time." (Eccl. 3:11.) These pictures may be used as the leader presents the verse, or they may be hung up with others and

on a long strip of heavy tan wrapping paper

the child asked to find a picture which illustrates the verse. They may be spread out and slips of paper with verses written on them may be given to the children. Each child chooses a picture to match his verse and brings both to the front of the room. The children then read the verses and show the pictures, explaining their choice. To carry this farther, the pictures may be pasted on a frieze and the verse pasted under them. Each child does his own pasting and so takes part in the making of the frieze. The frieze may be made of a long strip of heavy tan wrapping paper or wall paper.

In working out the above lesson the verses should be carefully chosen to tie up with other work the children are doing. They may all be about Jesus if the children are studying his life. They may be Thanksgiving verses at Thanksgiving time. In connection with a nature unit the thought of God's beautiful world may be brought out through these verses and pictures. By grouping verses under various headings it is possible to centralize the thought of the experience into some such summary as: Jesus loved people. God gave us a beautiful world. He has given us much to be thankful for.

The next step might be for the children to draw pictures to illustrate their verses. These might be made into posters, added to the frieze, or used to make a booklet or new frieze. A group of verses might be chosen to go with each unit as it is taught; by interpreting these in as many ways as possible and by referring back to them often the children will learn them without conscious effort.

Suggestions for Illustrations

1. Make collection of pictures
2. Make original pictures
3. Make a frieze
4. Make a poster
5. Make a scene in a box top
6. Make a booklet of questions answered by Bible verses and illustrated with the pictures the children draw
7. Dramatize a Bible verse (impromptu dramatization)
8. Illustrate a map, using Bible verses
9. Make a set of slides illustrating verses (see page 103)
10. Illustrate with blueprints
11. Write stories about verses
12. Choose verses to match the stories used in the department

BLUEPRINTING BIBLE STORIES. Children tire of drawing pictures and coloring them with crayons, if they are asked to do it over and over again. By letting them blueprint their illustrations occasionally there will be less monotony and the results will be unusual and interesting. Children enjoy experimenting with new materials and they like blueprinting.

Let us pretend that the story is that of Joseph. The teacher tells the lesson portion as vividly as possible, paying particular attention to descriptions, and the making of simple but distinct word pictures. The children must be able to visualize the desert tent, the flowing robes of Jacob, and the boyish figure of Joseph. They must see the group of disgruntled brothers, watching enviously as the father hands Joseph the brightly hued coat.

After the story is told discuss it with the children. Ask them to close their eyes and pretend they were with Joseph. What would they see? What kind of home did Joseph live in? Was it like the tents that are used nowadays for camping? What trees might they see? Where would they get their drinking water? What animals would be there?

Use pictures in connection with this discussion and call the children's attention to mass forms and shapes of objects for blueprinting in silhouette work. Let the children pose for several picture ideas. A few draperies are useful things to have on hand for such purposes as well as for costuming the spontaneous dramatization. This posing or forming living pictures gives the class a feeling for form and grouping, and will make the story more real and help to impress it upon the minds of the children.

Give a piece of paper the size of the piece of blueprint paper to each child and ask him to draw his version of the story, warning him that only shapes would show on the finished blueprint, and that objects should not be drawn one over the other. Groups of trees and people may be used in one drawing, but one object cannot be drawn over another.

Remember that the figures will be white on a deep blue background. A strip of paper should be cut for the ground and the other objects arranged on this. The whole drawing can be cut out in one piece or each object cut separately and pasted lightly on the piece of glass used in blueprinting. Tell the children there can be no lines drawn in any object. Shape is everything; the only way to produce lines is by cutting out little slivers of the paper, or by using a blue-colored pencil after the print is finished.

In a small class when the teacher has plenty of time, each child may make and blueprint his own picture. When time is a major consideration and where the teacher's aim is largely to promote a spirit of co-operation, the entire group of children may be working on one picture, each responsible for one part of it. In this type of work the child should draw his own picture and then be allowed to use different figures from other children's work. In this way each child feels that he has made a definite contribution to the picture. The children then arrange the parts on the glass, each with a tiny dab of paste to hold it in place.

Once the parts are arranged and pasted on, each child may use the picture and make his own print to take home or put in his individual notebook. In the making of a group picture you will find valuable lessons in co-operation and learning to contribute to the general good. On the other hand, in illustrating a long story like the story of Joseph, or in illustrating a group of Bible verses as a project in memorization, each child can illustrate a single scene or a single verse and then all the parts can be put together into a single booklet. Blueprints look very well mounted on brown wrapping paper. Children love to take things home to share with father and mother. Be sure to put a print in the Class Diary.

BIBLE VERSES

THE FOLLOWING verses are suggestive. It is a good thing for each leader to have a list in his notebook.

1. The earth is full of the loving-kindness of the Lord. (Psalms 33:5b.)
2. Your heavenly Father knoweth that ye have need of all these things. (Matt. 6:32b.)
3. He careth for you. (1 Peter 5:7b.)
4. A friend loveth at all times. (Proverbs 17:17a.)
5. The Lord hath done great things for us, whereof we are glad. (Psalms 126:3.)
6. Teach me thy way, O Lord. (Psalms 86:11a.)
7. I will praise thee, O Lord, with my whole heart. I will shew forth all thy marvellous works. (Psalms 9:1.)
8. Thou hast put gladness in my heart. (Psalms 4:7a.)
9. Let us do good unto all. (Gal. 6:10.)
10. None of us liveth to himself. (Rom. 14:7.)
11. He hath made everything beautiful in its time. (Eccl. 3:11.)
12. Bear ye one another's burdens and so fulfill the law of Christ. (Gal. 6:2.)
13. The earth is full of thy riches. (Psalms 104:24c.)
14. A new commandment I give unto you, that ye love one another. (John 13:34.)
15. Oh come, let us sing unto the Lord. (Psalms 95:1.)
16. While the earth remaineth, seedtime and harvest, and cold and heat, and summer and winter, and day and night shall not cease. (Gen. 8:22.)
17. For lo, the winter is past, the rain is over and gone. The flowers appear on the earth: the time of the singing of birds is come, and the voice of the turtle is heard in our land. The fig tree putteth forth her green figs, and the vines with the tender grape give a good smell. (Song of Sol. 2:11-13.)
18. The words of a talebearer are as wounds. (Prov. 18:8.)
19. A man that hath friends must shew himself friendly. (Prov. 18:24.)
20. A good name is rather to be chosen than great riches, and loving favour rather than silver and gold. (Prov. 22:1.)

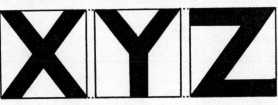

PART FOUR

AS SEASONS COME AND GO

The Dandelion Seed

I AM a Dandelion Seed
  The wind blew me away
I went with the wind
The wind blew me on the grass
The leaves fell on me
They kept me safe
They kept me warm
They hid me.

THE snow fell and covered me
  It kept me warm.
Spring came and the rain came tumbling down
The sun came out and shone and shone
It shone on me.
I started to grow.
I opened my bud.
I was a yellow dandelion. I looked like a little sun.
God sent the rain and the sun
He made me grow.
God sent the wind to carry me away.
Thank God for everything

A group of boys and girls pretended that they were dandelion seeds and wrote the story of their adventures. They wondered what kind of prayer dandelion seeds would pray if they could talk and think as boys and girls. They made their story and prayer sound like a poem.

PART FOUR

AS SEASONS COME AND GO

MANY OF OUR ACTIVITIES revolve about the holidays and seasons. This is particularly true in the kindergarten, primary and junior departments. The wise teacher will take this into consideration in planning his work. It is important to remember that handwork adapted to the season must be worth doing. If the children decide to make tray cards for the hospital (and hospitals always are glad of attractive tray cards for the holidays) then the activity has purpose and is permissible.

One wise superintendent took time during the summer vacation to plan handwork, based largely on seasonal activities, for the entire year. If the superintendent does plan activities in this way he should make it very clear that the program is a flexible one, which the class teacher may accept, change or discard, according to his judgment. The superintendent should evaluate the activities he suggests, choosing only the ones which are suitable and worth doing. He will confer with the teachers, being ready to help them when they need it.

We can roughly divide the year into four seasons: autumn, winter, spring, and summer.

1. *Autumn*
   A. The school situation
      a. Beginning school (What would Jesus expect of a boy or girl going to school for the first time? How can we show the teacher and other children we are God's children?)
      b. School problems (This is for older children. What relationship should there be between pupils, between pupil and teacher, between school and child?)
      c. Appreciation of school
      d. Plans for making teacher and other pupils happy
   B. October's "bright blue weather"
      a. Appreciation for the beauty of October
      b. Worship program planned about God, the Master Artist
   C. God's plans and preparation for winter
      a. Seed dispersal
      b. Migration of birds

   c. Hibernation of toads, insects, and animals

   d. Storing of winter food by squirrels

   e. Man's preparation for winter in Pilgrim times and now (Bring out that man has learned to work with God)

  D. November and Thanksgiving

   a. The harvest, God's gift of food (This is a continuation of the work started in October)

   b. The first Thanksgiving

   c. Giving thanks today

   d. Making others thankful

   e. The Thanksgiving worship service

2. *Winter*

  A. December and Christmas

   a. The Christmas story

   b. Appreciation of Christmas stories, poems, songs, pictures

   c. Creation of original Christmas stories, poems, songs, and pictures

   d. Making others happy at Christmas time

   e. Christmas around the world

   f. The making of the Christmas crèche

   g. The Christmas play

   h. The Christmas worship service

  B. January and World Friendship

   a. The New Year, a new start, resolutions, taking stock

   b. World Friendship month (World Friendship should underlie the work for all the months, but it is well to set aside one month for special emphasis when some definite unit of activity is taken up.)

   c. Washington (God sends the right person in times of need. God has given us a beautiful country. God expects us to be good citizens. What is a good citizen?)

3. *Spring*

  A. The awakening of nature

  B. Spring miracles

  C. God's goodness as shown in the springtime

  D. Easter

   a. Easter hope

   b. The first Easter

   c. Making others happy at Easter

   d. The Easter play, tableau, verse-reading choir

   e. The Easter worship service

  E. Mother's Day

   a. Giving God thanks for mothers

   b. Showing Mother we love her and want her to be happy

4. *Summer*

  A. Promotion

   a. What does promotion mean?

   b. Preparing ourselves for promotion

   c. Summarizing the accomplishments of the department or class and sharing some of the experiences with others

B. Summer months
    a. Learning more about God's wonderful world
    b. Sharing our discoveries with others
    c. Expressing our appreciation
    d. Our own summer worship service
C. Learning some of God's plans for his world
    a. The seed cycle
    b. Making cuttings of geraniums, etc., to show one of God's miracles
    c. The rain cycle
    d. Sun and moon and stars; God's plan for his universe
    e. Worship service, based on our discoveries

AUTUMN ACTIVITIES

The School Situation

Discuss with the children the beginning of school and let them tell some of their pleasant school experiences. Bring up the following questions:—

1. Why do boys and girls go to school?

2. Who gives them a school to go to, paying for books, paper, and teachers?

3. What does the teacher do for them?

4. What makes school a happy place or an unhappy place?

5. What can boys and girls do to make it happier?

Tell the children about the kind of school Jesus went to, and work out an imaginary story showing what kind of boy he must have been in order to have people say that he grew "in wisdom, in stature, and in favor with God and man."

If Jesus were a boy now, and if he went to school with them, what kind of boy would he be? Suggest several typical school problems and discuss how Jesus would probably meet those problems. These could be written down by the teacher for the class book.

Suggested Activities

1. After telling the children that a Christian is a person who takes Jesus as a model and tries to be like him, let the children work out a *set of rules governing school behavior* for a Christian boy or girl. Let them give reasons for making these rules.

> *Examples:* We should not whisper in school because it disturbs our neighbors.
> We should be careful coming down stairs, for if we push someone might fall.

He hath made everything beautiful in its time. (Ecclesiastes 3:11.)

Children choose Bible verses and draw pictures

2. *Planning Surprises*

a. Make a cutting of a begonia or geranium to take to school to make the room brighter. This could be done during the activity period in church school. One fairly large begonia can be cut up into many slips which should be rooted in wet sand. The following Sunday the slips might be transplanted into small paper or clay pots. Ruffled containers can be made, using bright-colored crepe paper and Scotch tape.

3. *Make a model of Friendly School* of cardboard, crepe paper, etc. See the miniature scene (page 77) for suggestions as to how to make trees, buildings, etc.

Make a set of rules governing one's conduct at Friendly School. These might be based on such problems as:—

1. When a new pupil comes to school
2. My friend of a different color
3. My friend from another land
4. When my classmate is in trouble

The children might draw pictures to illustrate these rules.

4. *Making a school prayer.* This may be dictated by the group to the teacher, who writes it down, or individual children may write their own school prayers.

To make these activities purposeful the leader will see that the problems are those which the children actually have to face in their everyday school

He giveth snow like wool; he scattereth the hoar-frost like ashes. He casteth forth his ice like morsels. (Psalms 147:16, 17.)

to make a frieze of the four seasons

life. He will also make a strong connection between Christian living and everyday school problems. The children should see that religion is not only a Sunday matter, but that the principles learned on Sunday should carry over into weekday living.

  5. *Reading and Discussion*

  a. Read Helen Hunt Jackson's poem "October's Bright Blue Weather." Also read her poem, "The Goldenrod is Yellow." Discuss the poem with the group, showing them pictures of autumn beauties of foliage and flowers. Ask them to bring in some of the beautiful leaves to press and hang on the screen. This is adaptable to the third and fourth-grade level.

  b. Make a miniature farm scene showing a country scene in autumn. See "The Miniature Scene," page 77.

A Unit about God's Plans for Winter

Begin this unit with a story. In the primary department the story might be based upon the following outline.

The Discoverers

  A. John and Jean move from the city into the country during the summer.

B. They become interested in

1. The animals on the farm:
   a. Woodchucks
   b. Squirrels
   c. Frogs
2. The birds
   a. Barn swallows
   b. Crows
   c. Robins
3. The insects
   a. Grasshoppers
   b. Crickets
   c. Bees
4. The garden

C. They become worried for the safety of the creatures in winter.

D. They discover that some animals and insects store up food for the winter, that some hibernate, and that many of the insects lay eggs that are hidden away throughout the winter under snow and ice. They learn that the insect-eating birds fly south where food is plentiful, and that the seed-eaters who can find food during the winter remain all year. They learn that some plants continue to live during the winter and in the spring send forth leaves and flowers while others make many seeds which are scattered far and wide in many interesting ways.

It is brought home to them that God has made definite plans for the continuing of his creatures and plants and that these plans are very wonderful.

Such a story as this makes a good start for the unit. The story may be broken up into several parts, with activities planned for each Sunday to fit

For, lo, the winter is past, the rain is over and gone;
The flowers appear on the earth; the time of the singing of birds is
come. (The Song of Solomon 2:11, 12.)

The frieze reminds the children that God is the Creator and loving Father

the part of the story told. More activities have been suggested than can be carried out by any one teacher in any one year, but variety will give scope for choice.

Suggested Activities

1. Animal Chart (primary or junior activity). See Charts, page 53.

2. The Bird Map (junior activity). See Map Making, page 64, for map suggestions.

3. Grasshopper and Cricket Cage (primary or junior activity). See Nature Activities, page 109.

4. Garden Activities. See Nature Activities, page 110.

5. Migrant Map. See Map Making, page 65.

THANKSGIVING

The activities mentioned already in the various fall units can be continued up to Thanksgiving and be brought to a climax at that time. If the one on God's plans for winter is used, another section dealing with man's use of God's plans may be added. This would include a discussion of the harvest. In the olden times a settler was dependent on the amount he could store away for the winter. If there was a poor harvest, or if some calamity such as fire destroyed his harvest, it was a very serious matter.

In these days of refrigerator cars, quick transportation, and widespread areas from which food can be sent we are not really alive to the real bounty

While the earth remaineth, seedtime and harvest, and cold and heat, and summer and winter, and day and night shall not cease. (Genesis 8:22.)

of all people. His abundant care is seen in the world of nature.

of God's gifts of sun, rain, and favorable growing conditions. Stories of the past and projects built about the importance of the harvest will give the children a small idea of how much they have to be grateful for.

Naturally the story of the Pilgrims and the first American Thanksgiving should be told as realistically and dramatically as possible. We must not forget that to children it is not a many-times-told story as it is to adults. We can make it vital and new.

Stories of the migrant pickers who harvest the great crops today may be told, and creative activities worked out from the stories.

"Feeding America" can be developed into a worth-while unit.

In all these units the child should be taught to recognize the mind and heart of God at work from the past to the present and ready to extend into the future.

The idea of God as creator and the great present force upon which we depend is one we want to keep always before the pupils. Another thought to emphasize is that we are seekers after ways of living and working in harmony with God's rules.

We want to demonstrate that there are many new things about these great laws that are being discovered all the time, and that as scientists of the future, children must learn to work with God in using the powers God has put into the world.

Activities

1. *The Pilgrim Scene.*
2. *Prayers.*
3. *The Thanksgiving Litany.*
4. *Miniature Scene*—Autumn on the Farm.

CHRISTMAS

The Crèche

Legend tells us that Saint Francis of Assisi wished to make the Christmas story more real to a group of Italian peasants in the district where he taught. He chose a beautiful woman and baby to represent the mother and child. To these he added a little donkey, sheep, lambs, and doves to complete his living picture. These he grouped beautifully in a stable, and hundreds of people came to see, admire, and worship.

One activity that children love is to present the Christmas tableau. Combined with a story, music, and poetry, it forms a lovely center for a Christmas worship service.

Italy and France had many wood carvers in the Middle Ages. Not long after St. Francis created his first crèche, an artist of that day thought of carving the scene out of wood. Later clay, wax, and porcelain were used in making the Christmas scene and it became the usual thing to have beautiful elaborate crèches in the churches and homes of the people. The custom was such a lovely one and gave such opportunity for artistic development that it spread rapidly.

Exquisite crèches have been made by real artists, and thousands of dollars have been spent on them. The custom has been taken to other countries. We see crude pottery crèches from Central America, plaster ones made for sale in dime stores, beautiful porcelain ones made to be sold in specialty shops.

The joy of creation is a keen joy, and we should help our pupils to develop whatever artistic power they have. If their work is sincere, then it is of value, no matter how crude. Crèches can be made of different materials.

For directions for making Christmas crèches, see the Miniature Scene and Diorama. Page 79.

Baby Christmas Trees. See How to Make Trees. Miniature Scene and Diorama, page 87.

The Birds' Christmas Tree. See Nature Activities, page 107.

Christmas Transparencies. See page 115.

Christmas Cards. See Greeting Cards, page 40.

Gifts. See page 145.

It is well to order a few more copies of the weekly story paper than you have pupils. These extra ones, and those the children have read and are willing to give back, can be cut up and the stories, poems, puzzles, and pictures mounted on cards or folders to be sent to the children's ward of the hospital. These should be bright and attractive. Using one or two stories for each folder is better than making heavy scrapbooks, for little hands are weak and heavy things difficult to hold. Besides, one large scrapbook would entertain only one child at a time, while the same material made into fifteen booklets or cards would keep fifteen children entertained.

SPRINGTIME

FROM THE TIME the first pussy willow sheds its winter wrappings until spring merges into summer, the wonder and appreciation for new life and new miracles should be stressed. This is especially true in the kindergarten and primary departments, but juniors, too, should be led to feel the beauty and wonder of the change of season, and to realize that here again God shows his world that he may be depended upon. Genesis 8:22 shows that even in ancient days people realized this.

The message of Easter is a difficult one to deal with in teaching children; there is so much we do not understand ourselves; there are so many conflicting beliefs. The thought of death is alien to a child's understanding. Until the need arises and he begins to question it is better to refrain from emphasizing this serious side of Easter.

This is especially true with kindergarten and primary children. Easter should not be shadowed by Good Friday's pain and sorrow.

This means that the creative activities chosen for the Easter season should be happy ones connected with the miracles of rebirth and awakening to be observed in nature.

1. Easter Cards.

Activities for Kindergarten

These should be very simple. After talking about the return of the birds, the opening of flowers, the change from caterpillar to butterfly, let the children draw an Easter card.

Provide an envelope for this to help carry the illusion that this is a real card and a gift for some loved person.

For Primary and Junior Children

Various techniques may be used. A study of Easter cards from former years will give suggestions and help them to decide what they would like to do. Encourage them to create their own designs rather than copy those of others. Specimens are intended to be suggestive only. See page 40 for suggestions for making greeting cards.

2. The Easter Diorama.

This is primarily a junior or intermediate activity though the upper primary classes can work out simple ones as well. See page 68 for suggestions on the miniature scene and on dioramas.

3. Experimenting with Propagation. See Nature Activities, page 110.

4. Creative Writing. See page 12.

a. Develop a litany with the children based on the wonders of spring.
b. Write a class poem.
c. Pretend you were a bulb and tell the story of your life from the time you were bought to Easter morning.
d. Write up Easter experiments for class book.

5. Pictorial Expression. See Illustration by Drawing, page 47.

a. Draw a picture of the decorated front of the church on Easter.
b. Draw a church-school worship center.
c. Draw children doing something to make someone happy on Easter.
d. Draw the window of a florist shop with children looking into it.
e. Draw an Easter frieze.
f. Illustrate the articles you have written in the class book.

6. The Diorama or Miniature Scene.

a. People buying flowers in a greenhouse or florist shop.
b. An illustrated Bible verse, such as "The flowers appear on the earth, the time of the singing of birds is come."
c. A worship center.

7. Living pictures. While this really belongs with dramatization, it is one of the creative activities, and should be mentioned briefly. If it is to have creative value the children should help decide what the picture is to be, how it is to be arranged, and they should also have a hand in the choosing and making of costumes. This activity is a good one for juniors and intermediates.

8. The Nature Museum. See Nature Activities, page 108.

MOTHER'S DAY

Suggestions for Creative Activity

1. Greeting Cards. See sections on Greeting Cards, page 40. These cards should have letters or verses written on them.

2. Decorated letters. Write letters to mothers and decorate them with sketches.

3. Original poems.

4. Plant holders. See diagram on page 112.

5. Garden markers. See diagram on page 112.

6. Potted plants. See diagram on page 112. Children make decorated pots or holders of crepe paper or cellophane.

7. Decorated prune bottles, or other glass jars. Cut flower from seed catalogue and glue it to bottle. Paint a colored border at the top of the jar. Shellac the jar.

8. Decorated wooden box.

9. Seed envelopes. Make envelopes from brown wrapping paper. Children draw flower pictures on outside and color them. Print the name of the seeds on the outside. The teacher buys poppy, zinnia, or marigold seeds by the ounce and divides them among the children. Perhaps someone with a garden will donate seed.

10. Promise Cards. Plan and discuss something each child can do to make his mother happier. Make sure it is something possible and that the child really wants to do it.

Children decorate cards and write their promises on them.

The teacher should check later to see if the children fulfilled their promises.

CHILDREN'S DAY

Children's Day is the climax of the year's studies. Bibles are presented, promotions made, and diplomas issued. Usually there is some recognition made of the work the children have done during the year. There is special music and often some type of dramatic presentation. On Children's Day parents, children, and church are drawn closer together. It is the church school's golden opportunity to show the parents what is being done for their children, and to enlist their interest and co-operation.

It seems an excellent chance to have some type of exhibit of the children's work. This may be set up in some one general room or in the various department rooms, the latter for preference, so that the parents can see the environment in which their children study. In carrying out such an exhibit it is important that the articles exhibited should be the outgrowth of activities actually worked out in connection with the work carried on during the year, and not just a pretty display made up for the occasion.

If the children have carried out certain Golden Rule projects illustrated accounts should be displayed. Pages from the class book (see page 55) will give the parents a bird's-eye view of the whole year in review. Maps, charts, dioramas, friezes, illustrated Bible material, activities connected with various units, all tell a story of progress and of worth-while activity.

Several children should be appointed to remain with the exhibit for the half hour preceding church and others for a few minutes after church. The children should write invitations to their parents, asking them to visit the exhibit. The planning connected with this exhibit should be carried out by the children, working with the teachers and superintendent. They should be encouraged to make suggestions, and to help set the articles out attractively. They should write out any necessary explanations. The more they put into their work the more educational values will they derive from it.

Guard against the feeling among children that they are showing how smart they are and how well they have done. Encourage rather the feeling that here is their chance to share their discoveries and the nice things they have with interested friends and parents. The exhibit may be arranged in several ways. Unity will be achieved if objects are arranged according to seasonal activities, units, or the months of the year.

Be sure that the parents understand why certain things are done. You may let the children make paper dolls illustrating the characters in some World Friendship book. People seeing paper dolls without knowing why they were made would naturally jump to the conclusion that time was being wasted. If, however, those paper dolls were used in some little dramatization carried out on the top of a table, or if they were made to illustrate the type of costume made in some other land, or to make the story more real, their existence is justified. The teacher also should have explanations attached to any object that might be misunderstood.

A six-year-old's drawing is something else that a word of explanation might help make clear. Some of them look like rainbows run riot and need to be interpreted.

Besides showing fathers and mothers what the children have been learning and doing during the year, the planning for and arrangement of such an exhibit serves as an excellent review of the year's activities for the children themselves. It is a record of real progress, improvement, and growth.

We Think of Others

MANY OF THE ACTIVITIES of the church school center about giving, sharing, or making something for others. "God loveth a cheerful giver," "It is more blessed to give than to receive," "Freely ye have received, freely give," and "As ye would that men should do to you, do ye also to them like-wise," are not simply verses to learn by rote. They must be learned by heart and the only way to learn them by heart is to practice them. The pleasant glow that comes to a child from doing something for someone else makes the child want to repeat the pleasant sensation. Deriving satisfaction, he wants to do more. By giving him opportunity to serve he learns the joy of service, a habit is formed, and a principle of living is established.

One primary group had a series of discussions about the money they brought each Sunday. Some thought they were paying to come to school as they did to go to the movies. One child had a vague idea that the money went to the superintendent. Still others thought it was given to God, but had no idea how he received it or for what he spent it.

Then the leader told the children that the money was brought to give happiness to people who were unhappy, to help those in need, and to help pay for the running of the church. A list of things for which the money could be used was written on the blackboard and afterward copied into the class book. Some of the items were:—

1. Send money to the Grenfell Mission to buy medicines for the people in Labrador. (The children had just heard a story about Dr. Grenfell.)

2. Send a Christmas box to children in another part of the country.

3. Send a magazine to a member of the church who is an invalid.

4. Take fruit to a blind member of the church.

5. Send money to China to feed children who are hungry.

During the discussion it was brought out that we do not give money directly to God, but we use it for things which he would like to have done. The leader told the class that Jesus once said that when we did things for others it was just the same as doing them for him.

One group made up their own offering verse to use during the offering service:—

OUR GIFTS

Dear Father, our love we are bringing,
Our gifts to others and you,
We hope it will make you happy,
And make others happy, too.

"It would be nice if we could sing it," suggested one child.

Fortunately the pianist could do a great deal more than play the piano. She collected a little group of the best singers and together they made up a tune to fit the words. The entire activity was most worth while.

In another group the gift was a class affair. Each class chose a project and each had its own bank. One class saved for a much needed wastebasket for the department. Their aim was to help keep the primary room as beautifully clean as God's house should be kept. The wastebasket was presented as a surprise during a worship service arranged by the boys who had saved for it. The custodian of the church loved children and had been a real friend of the primary department. The class had been told the story of Samuel helping Eli in the church, and they felt that they were doing as he did.

Several years later a small group of boys and girls took it upon themselves to see that papers were picked up, chairs shoved into place, and pencils and other supplies put away. As promotion time drew near the leader said, "I don't know what I am going to do without my good helpers. I'll miss them so."

The following Sunday John took his little brother to school and was instructing him concerning the care of the room. When everything was in order he brought his brother up and introduced him.

"I'm training him to take my place," he said. "He's six years old and he will be in here next year."

"I can do it," promised the six-year-old valiantly. He did.

Service Activities

Service activities may be divided roughly into two classes, doing things for others and making gifts to others. Services that the children can perform to make others happy belong in the first class and the second class includes the act of giving.

VISITS

One group of children became interested in a blind member of a church. The teacher of the group took his entire class to visit this woman one Sunday. They sang her their newest song, recited a poem, and talked with her. When they returned to the church they were bubbling over with the joy that their experience had given both to them and to her. The superintendent happened to be at the farther side of the room when they returned and they almost threw themselves upon her in their eagerness to tell what had happened.

"She cried for joy," one exclaimed in wonder, and the others echoed, "Yes, she cried for joy."

This initial visit was the forerunner of many others. They took her gifts of flowers on her birthday, a valentine in February, and a Christmas present. In turn she showed them her watch, read Braille, and pricked a message for them in Braille which was promptly pasted into their class book. This group of children practiced kindness and thought for another and found the experience such a happy one that they wanted to repeat it.

Not far away was a home for blind women. One junior group of children put together a program of Christmas carols and poems with which to entertain these blind women one evening shortly before Christmas. This, too, was a happy occasion. For several years different groups of children kept up this entertainment, and the women looked forward to their visit.

Sometimes it is possible to take groups of children to institutions such as the Day Nursery. They learn about these from first-hand observation and their interest and sympathy are aroused. In connection with these visits they should always be given an opportunity to do something to make the recipients happier. They might take a plant to one of the homes for adults, or a doll or toy to the Day Nursery.

Certain rules should govern the making of these visits, and these should be discussed with the children before they start out. Let the children formulate their own rules and give their reasons for such rules. These might read:—

1. On the way to —— we must stay close together.
2. We must be orderly in the street and not call people's attention to us.
3. We must be polite so that —— will want us to come again.
4. We must be careful in crossing streets.
5. We must do our best to give pleasure to those we are going to visit.

There are certain regulations which the teacher or superintendent in charge will follow. Below is a tentative list.

1. The teacher will make the arrangements first, making sure that the proposed visit is a welcome one. He will make sure of the exact time and tell how many he is expecting to bring.

2. Two adults or more should go, depending on size of group.

3. The leader should keep the group together and be especially careful in crossing streets.

4. He will insist on perfect obedience and orderly conduct.

5. He will get the group back to the church safely and then to their homes if it is an evening affair.

GIFTS

Presents are always fun to give and fun to get. They make pleasant expressions of friendliness and are much to be encouraged. There is a great variety of presents a class or department can give, ranging from an entire Christmas dinner supplied by the whole department for a family who would go without otherwise to a simple little gift a child might make for his mother or father or friend.

Some gifts may be bought. A class might save its money and buy some desirable object to present to the rest of the church-school department; perhaps candlesticks and candles for the worship center, a new book on world friendliness for the department library, a lovely picture for their own room or for another department. It may be a book or a picture to send to one of the southern mountain schools, or to a school for Negro children. The children should first know the need or the desire for the gift. They should want to give something definite with a certain goal in view.

Sometimes classes carry out their own ideas for individual gifts, and sometimes a whole department combines in making a gift. A primary group was planning a play that called for a small undecorated Christmas tree. After talking the matter over with their leader it was decided that after the tree was used in church it should be sent to make some family happy. All the children in the department were having trees at home, but one of the children knew of a family that was not planning to have one.

The result was that the entire department combined to give this family a real Christmas. The children saved their money for the tree and its decorations and a gift for each member of the family. Committees of children bought the ornaments, and gifts. After the play the tree was dressed up so that they might see how pretty it was and the gifts were put around it. This might well be the center of a service of worship stressing the joy of making others happy.

If gifts are to be purchased let the children help in shopping for them. The gifts seem more real if they can be handled. Also let the children help to pack and send the box. A small class may go shopping with the teacher; in a large group a committee of children should be chosen to do this.

In rural churches, or if stores are too far away, a catalogue from a large mail-order house may serve as a store and the entire group discuss and choose the gift, order it, and enjoy the added thrill of having it come to them through the mail.

GIFTS FOR CHILDREN

Gifts may be made for children who are ill, and for children in hospitals.

1. *Scrapbooks*

    a. Picture scrapbooks.
    b. Story and poem scrapbooks.
    c. Scrapbooks of games, puzzles, and suggestions of things to be done.

These scrapbooks may be made of heavy brown wrapping paper. Loose-leaf notebooks, or commercial scrapbooks may also be used. For hospital use many small ones with several pictures, stories, and poems are better than large ones, for they are easier to hold, they serve more children at one time, and more children can be at work on them at the same time.

2. *Puzzles, Using Pictures*

Pictures may be mounted on tough but not brittle cardboard, heavy paper, or wood, taking care to spread the glue or paste smoothly over the entire surface. Primary children do the paper and cardboard ones best for they can be cut with heavy scissors. Juniors enjoy working with jig saw and can make good wooden puzzles. These may be put into decorated envelopes or boxes. Let the children think up a good title for each one they make and write it on the outside.

3. *The T. Puzzle*

(See diagram below) This is a good puzzle to use at parties or to send to hospitals. The children may trace the pattern, cut it out, and put it into an envelope. On the outside of the envelope they may write the following:—

> Here are some pieces
> That make up a T
> It may look simple,
> But try it and see.

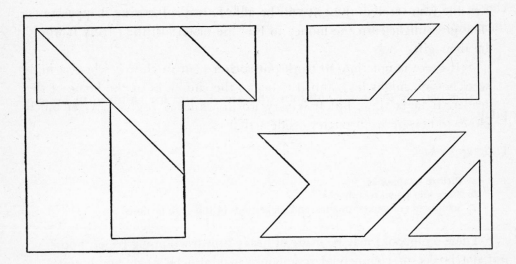

4. *The Crossword Puzzle*

Children may save crossword puzzles from newspapers and mount them with their clues on wrapping paper. These may be sent to hospitals or recreation centers at camps.

5. *Paper-Doll Kits*

Little girls love paper dolls and will enjoy preparing paper-doll kits to send to sick classmates, orphanages, or hospitals. Dolls with outspread arms are best. These are used as patterns. Each girl should have one doll and a dress or two to send; each should have an envelope large enough to hold doll, wardrobe, paper, and perhaps a box of colored pencils.

The filled envelopes should contain:—

a. Doll.
b. Several heavy paper patterns for dresses, coats, pajamas, and other accessories.
c. Several costumes made up by the givers to show the recipients how to make clothes.
d. Pieces of colored construction paper, wall paper, and white paper to use in making clothes.
e. A pencil with an eraser.
f. A box of colored crayons or colored pencils.

The value of the making up of such a kit lies in the fact that there is so much work the giver may put into it. Also the work is not all finished; the one who receives the gift will be able to use it for many happy hours. The girls might earn the money to buy the materials; then truly it would be their gift.

If there is not time to work out such a plan in church school a mid-week session might be planned either at the church or at the home of the leader. It takes time, but it is very worth while. A leader can get much closer to her group through outside activities.